THE FRENCH BAKER

SÉBASTIEN BOUDET

THE FRENCH BAKER

AUTHENTIC RECIPES FOR TRADITIONAL BREADS, DESSERTS, AND DINNERS

TRANSLATED BY VERONICA CHOICE

PHOTOGRAPHER CARL KLEINER   ILLUSTRATOR OLAF HAJEK   ART DIRECTOR JUSTINE LAGACHE

SKYHORSE PUBLISHING

WHY I WOULD NEVER WRITE A BOOK

I've always said that I would never write a cookbook. A recipe is a live being to me, with a soul that continuously changes and evolves. In my own recipe books, I have crossed sections out, written notes and comments, and made corrections all over the place.

Over the years, I have worked, baked, and cooked food in many different countries, and I've learned the hard way that recipes are not worth much if you don't understand the processes behind them. Proportions can vary depending on how you bake or cook, where you bake or cook, or simply based on what kind of ingredients you use.

My biggest concern about publishing my recipes in a book has been: How will my wonderful recipes live on and continue to grow and evolve if they are written down in a finished book? How can I influence the dish when the book finally ends up in the reader's hands? How can I help the cook or baker if things go wrong, if the results are unsuccessful, or if they simply don't work? Thankfully, all my questions were answered when I took up blogging.

A small stone in a sourdough bread loaf and an angry customer turned out to be my reasons for starting my blog; so now, you, my reader, can have a direct link to me via my blog at www.brodpassion.se. Here, you can follow my everyday experiences and get extra materials in the form of pictures, blog commentary, and recorded recipes. Not even I know what my blog will have in the future. But through my blog, I know I will be able to influence my book long after it has been published.

Crafting this book was a journey—both figuratively and literally. During the fall of 2011, I went with some of the people who have been involved in this project to beautiful Pau in the south of France. Our goal was to cook food, eat, document, write, and—most importantly—be inspired. Now, many miles later, the book is finally finished.

The French Baker is about love for delicious sourdough bread and for the great foods we eat, but most of all, it is about love for humanity. Because in my life, that's where great food begins.

SEBASTIEN

SOURDOUGH SCHOOL

I have always been fascinated by the fact that so many people bake. But even with all this passion and dedication to the craft, it seems to me as though there is a lack of knowledge about basic ingredients among both professionals and those who bake at home. Today, you can find recipes everywhere, and it's easy to forget what matters the most: the soul of the recipe and a genuine understanding of its ingredients. All you really need to make great tasting bread is flour, salt, and water. Once you understand the function of each ingredient, your bread will taste even better, you'll be more successful each time you bake, and you'll find the process to be much more enjoyable.

YEAST OR SOURDOUGH?

This has been a hot topic of discussion among professionals and bakers at home, and it has been covered extensively in many blogs, including my own. My preference is to almost always bake with sourdough. Baking with sourdough is about four aspects:

THE PHILOSOPHICAL ASPECT
THE CULINARY ASPECT
THE PRESERVABILITY ASPECT
THE HEALTH ASPECT

THE PHILOSOPHICAL ASPECT

The leavening of the sourdough is what I love the most. It gives me a sense of calm, a certain rhythm, and a feeling of freedom. Every time I mix sourdough, water, flour, and sea salt, millions of microorganisms are activated. Within this chaotic world, microorganisms simply try to do what they are programmed to: live, eat, reproduce, and tear down anything that gets in their way. The laws of nature rule here, and we humans are just the observers. The observer who wants to be an actor? Well, that's me, the sourdough baker.

I consider sourdough baking to be one of the most gratifying tasks there is. When my alarm clock goes off in the morning, my first thought is about my dough. These have been leavening during the night, working on their own, and are now waiting for me to bake with them.

Working with yeast is a totally different experience. Breads made with yeast have elements that have to be timed correctly and executed in a faster speed under more stressful circumstances. I consider this a disadvantage. However, many people try to turn this to their advantage, hoping to fit the baking process into their stressful lives, where the bread has to be finished within a few hours. I want to experience the complete opposite. The time and freedom that baking with sourdough allows me is robbed from me when I bake with yeast.

I have read many sourdough recipes that contain both yeast and sourdough. I don't understand why anyone would want to use yeast, which is made for quick baking, together with sourdough, which is specifically intended for slow baking. I think it's important to be consistent. There is a method out there for everyone—no matter which one it is—and you should choose your leavening method based on how much time you actually have available.

THE CULINARY ASPECT

The right leavening method depends entirely on which bread you want, for what purpose you intend to use it, and what kind of flavor and appearance you are after. Sourdough leavening takes time and results in deeper flavors—nothing new in that. I have never heard of a wine, a cheese, or vinegar that has exploded with flavor

13

after only thirty-five minutes. During the leavening process, flavors and aromas develop along with texture and porosity, and, of course, there will be a big difference in the end product depending on how long the dough has been leavening and in what manner. Sourdough is heavier and more compact, but also has a creamier crumb consistency; yeast offers a fluffier, lighter, and more airy consistency. The texture, taste, and color of the crumbs depend in large part on how the dough is mixed. You can achieve an airy sourdough bread with the help of a sturdy mixer, but by doing so you will lose some of the flavor. The crumbs of the sourdough bread also stay moist longer than bread that is made with yeast; this allows the crust of the sourdough bread to develop better. Bread that has been baked with yeast has a tendency to dry up quickly if it's baked for too long. (If you bake with yeast but want to bake it for a longer period of time to achieve a harder crust, you can always add fat to the dough—for example, olive oil, butter, pig or duck fat.)

THE SUSTAINABILITY ASPECT

There are two types of sustainability. I separate them into sustainability that allows the bread to stay fresh and tasty for several days and sustainability in relation to our planet and the quality of life of the farmer, the miller, and the baker. In twenty years, I want to be able to look my grandchildren—as well as all men and women who have decided to become bakers—in the eye and know that I have done everything I can to preserve our beautiful nature, our landscape, and—in the long run—my pride in this incredibly wonderful profession.

When baking with sourdough, it is important to use high-quality flour that contains plenty of essential microorganisms. By using more and more yeast in baking, we have created a negative spiral in which great and wholesome microorganisms are no longer important. This has resulted in the production of low-quality flour throughout the last fifty years. With lesser quality flour comes the need for adding ascorbic acid, alpha-amylases, or extra gluten to the flour, and in turn this affects the jobs of farmers and millers. Behind great flour, there are people who must make decisions regarding every aspect from seeds to flour: we're talking about the origins of the seeds, the seeding, fertilization, and the method of the milling.

A natural, high-quality flour demands more attention and knowledge than boring industrial flour that has been loaded with additives. If you want your bread to last longer and not turn dry as a desert after only a few hours, make sure to bake large loaves of bread. The leavening method isn't the only thing that plays a part in how long a loaf will last; the size of the bread matters, too. While bread made with yeast continuously loses quality—both visually and in taste—the flavor of sourdough bread continues to develop in various directions. Plus, the crust acts as a shield to protect the bread from losing moisture.

14

To sum it up: thick crust, large loaf, and sourdough make for bread that will last all week.

THE HEALTH ASPECT

Sourdough's extended leavening time not only gives the bread a better taste, but also makes it more nutritious. The reason sourdough leavening increases nutritional value is based on the antioxidant phytic acid. Phytic acid can be found in all grains, and in comparison to other antioxidants, it has a negative impact on other nutritional components. Phytic acid binds minerals and vitamins while preventing the body from absorbing the nutrition. In practice, this means that even if we eat ingredients that have plenty of nutritional value, the body is unable to absorb any of it.

A prolonged leavening of twelve hours or more breaks down the phytic acid; this means that when we eat the bread, all the bread's vitamins and minerals are released into our bodies. For many years, we have all just looked at the list of ingredients on the packaging without considering if our bodies will actually absorb any of the product's nutrition. Depending on the amount of phytic acid, there's actually a big difference between what we eat and what our bodies absorb.

My grandmother used to say that we have teeth for a reason and that it's important to chew our food thoroughly. Bread made with yeast is usually softer than sourdough and therefore we don't have to chew as much anymore. In conclusion: we have been baking bread for several thousands of years, and it wasn't so long ago that it was the main staple of our diet. Industrial yeast is a new chapter in the history of bread making and even if it sometimes serves a good purpose, it has negatively affected taste, longevity, health, and—on a more esoteric level—the philosophy behind what bread represents to mankind.

I think sourdough bread is the smart choice. I was brought up on the legends of Jean de La Fontaine and my thoughts wander to the story about the hare that challenges the turtle to a long distance race. As soon as the start signal sounds, the hare takes off at incredible speed. Pretty soon, the hare feels so confident that he has secured the victory that he lies down at the side of the road to take a nap. I am sure you remember what happens next . . . Slow and steady or quick but uneven?

To make great tasting bread, sourdough is an obvious choice for me. And you really just need three ingredients to bake it. With some water, flour, and salt, you can get a wonderful spectrum of texture, appearance, and taste—anything from a rich rye bread with a thick crust and a creamy interior to a simple but fresh baguette. Let's begin with the salt.

15

salt

The Orchestra Conductor

There are two main categories of salt: sea salt and mountain salt. Mountain salt is the white, fine grain salt that we can find in grocery stores. It's produced through excavations in salt mines and is washed by chemicals. In other words, mountain salt is refined. During the refining process, all nutrients such as magnesium, iron, calcium, and anything of nutritional value are washed away at the same time chemicals called anti-caking agents are added. Anti-caking agents probably aren't dangerous, but I question if they are something I want to have in my bread. It feels boring and unnatural.

I prefer to use coarse sea salt when I bake. Ninety-seven percent of the earth's water is salt water and it gives us unlimited resources. Natural sea salt is one of the "fruits" of the ocean, a fruit that we can enjoy without damaging the tree that carries it.

Sea salt has been produced in the same way for more than two thousand years, and whenever Jean-Antoine, my salt producer from Guérande in the west of France, tells me about the production process, I feel proud to know that I bake with his salt.

To produce natural sea salt, the sea water is transported, based on low and high tides, through shallow pools—called salines—and with help from the wind and sun, the water evaporates and leaves behind fine, porous salt crystals. To produce great tasting salt from the ocean takes time, love, and knowledge—pretty much the same as what is required to bake great tasting bread. But when you use natural sea salt, you get so much more in return.

The salt affects the gluten during the baking process and helps the dough become robust and elastic. If you forget to put salt in your dough, it will become sticky and will grab on to the table and your fingers.

Salt also allows the dough to hold on to more water for a longer period of time. The right amount of salt in bread also affects shelf life and moisture.

Salt activates the caramelizing of the bread during the baking and gives the crust its lovely brown color. Without salt, the bread would never turn brown in the oven.

Salt also enhances flavors and works as an aromatic catalyst. It doesn't add flavor, but rather enhances the ones that are already there.

Last but not least, salt stabilizes the leavening. During the leavening of sourdough, plenty of bacteria, enzymes, acids, and amylases are activated in the bread. All of these have their individual tasks to perform. Inside the dough, there is a whole world of activity and it is pretty chaotic. Salt can be compared to the conductor of an orchestra, who makes sure that each individual component performs the tasks they are supposed to, in the correct order, in the right way.

Now it's time to move on to the next important pillar within the art of bread making: water.

17

osmosis

The Ways of Water

Without knowledge of how water functions, it's difficult to make great bread. Water exists everywhere and it affects us in many different ways, but when you bake bread, it is osmosis that's the most important phenomenon to understand.

In simple terms, osmosis is the process that enables water to move in such a way that it will always spread to all available areas until it has done so evenly. The moist and the dry end up in balance and the concentration evens out. It's a fascinating and natural process that happens all on its own, and this phenomenon occurs all around us. It is osmosis that turns water and flour into dough, that allows salmon to be cured, or gives a macaroon that perfect, soft texture.

Osmosis allows you to add plenty of water to the flour so that it becomes really moist. Unfortunately, osmosis can also work against you. Since the air is always drier than the bread, moisture releases from the bread, and this can quickly dry out the loaf. Osmosis's quest for balance is basically what dries the bread out and makes it stale in only a few days.

There are, however, a few tricks for preserving the moisture in bread. For example, industrially manufactured bread is stored in plastic bags. But since the water in the bread evaporates, condensation is created in the bag, which makes for a moist environment. To ensure that the bread does not go bad, it is therefore necessary to make small holes in the bag. These little holes allow for small amounts of moisture to seep out of the bag, allowing the bread to last longer.

Sourdough bread is, however, stored most frequently in paper bags, as the crust of the bread is a natural protection against the evaporation of moisture. The thick crust works as a shield against the environment and keeps moisture inside the bread, giving it a longer shelf life. Sourdough bread usually lasts for a whole week, whereas yeast bread that has a thinner crust will last for a shorter period of time.

The phenomenon of osmosis helps us understand why it is important to have a thicker crust, why bread needs a proper autolysis (see page 41), and last but not least, why it is important to bake with a lot of water.

18

flour

Great Grains Equal Great Flour

Great crops equal great flour! Unfortunately, there are many bakers who have no idea where their flour comes from. The farmer cultivates his grain, the miller grinds his flour, the baker bakes his bread, and in between, there is the distributor. I wish the baker would spend a little more time out in the field to see and experience the ways in which his ingredients are cultivated and harvested. I wish that the miller would spend more time in bakeries to see how incredibly beautiful the baking of bread truly is.

Personally, I keep in close contact with the farmers that cultivate the wheat and rye that will eventually be the flour I use. Great grains equal great flour, and great flour equals great bread. If the plant in the field is healthy, it means that we ultimately get higher quality flour. The plants need space for the sun and the wind to reach their roots, and it's important that they're not sown too close together. The wind forces the plant to build a deeper network of roots to stand strong, and this deeper network of roots is the foundation by which a plant can absorb minerals through the water in the soil. If the farmer does not give the plant enough space to grow and instead substitutes nutrition with supplements from artificial watering and fertilizers, the roots will be shallower in the soil. The result is that the roots don't work their way down the soil to absorb real nutrition; ultimately this leaves us with weaker, less nutritious flour.

When baking, it's also important for the gluten to be of high quality. Gluten is a protein that keeps the dough together and makes it elastic. It operates as a web that binds the starch and gives the bread a nice interior. The gluten level differs from flour to flour; durum wheat and regular wheat, for example, have the highest levels of gluten, while graham flour and rye have lower levels of gluten. I often use flour with lower gluten levels, and in my opinion, you will achieve equally great results with less gluten if you adjust the baking process accordingly. By performing autolysis (see page 41) and gently kneading the dough, you lessen the need for flour that contains high levels of gluten.

GET TO KNOW YOUR FLOUR

The recipes in this book are based on three kinds of flour: wheat, durum wheat, and rye.

Regular wheat is produced by grinding the grain until only the kernel remains. Most of the vitamins, minerals, and enzymes can be found in the seed and husks, and since these are removed in regular wheat flour, the nutritional value is lower. The all-important protein (gluten) does, however, exist in the kernel, and these high levels of gluten make for increased baking capabilities.

20

Durum wheat has a harder kernel and an even higher protein level than regular wheat. It is more sensitive to cold and prefers to grow in warm climates, such as the Mediterranean and the lower regions of Arizona and California. Good quality durum flour has a strong yellow color. I like to add some durum wheat to my dough, as it adds a nice texture and good flavor.

Rye is a more robust grain that is more suitable to a colder climate. Since the husks are soft, it is easy to grind the whole grain with stone.

Rye is nutritious, but it also has a higher level of phytic acid since the husk is included in the flour. Good-quality rye also contains plenty of healthy fats.

Last but not least I would like to mention Spelt flour. It is an old variety that has been getting some new attention as of late, mostly due to the fact that it contains high levels of protein and is rich with minerals.

THE MILL ORGA

One day a few years ago, I decided to visit the mill that was grinding the flour I used for my baking. When I arrived, I realized that what I had been using was what I refer to as industrial flour—basically a flour filled with additives and produced at great speed, using grains sprayed with pesticides and cultivated with artificial fertilizers. In essence, it is grown without any love or care whatsoever.

When I was driving back to Stockholm, I felt like I had been completely fooled. It would be impossible for me to look my customers in the eyes again if I continued using this same flour at my bakery. I could not simply return and proclaim to everyone who had put their trust in me that I had any kind of quality control over my own ingredients. Thus, the hunt began. My goal was to find a mill that could grind flour with true passion and without any additives.

When I heard about the mill Orga, I immediately called Leif Nyman, who manages the mill with his brother Lennart: "Hi Leif, my name is Sébastien and I am a baker in Stockholm looking for great flour to use in my sourdou . . ." He hung up on me before I even had a chance to finish my sentence. I braced myself and dialed the number again, but I didn't even get a chance to speak before he hung up a second time. Stubborn as I am, I jumped in my car and drove over to the mill Orga. Once I got there, I asked Leif why he had hung up on me and he answered: "Shit. A damn baker from Stockholm! What about flour that sucks?" I later found out that he had tried to sell his flour to "fine bakers" in Stockholm for more than fifteen years, but had been told again and again that his flour was not good enough to bake with. There was no questioning his frustration—for the past fifteen years, they had been using an amazing 150-year-old stone mill to grind turkey, chicken, and rabbit feed! All the while I had been baking bread with industrial flour ground by a mill as big as a two-story house.

I left Orga mill with a couple of sacks containing the most beautiful wheat and rye flour imaginable, and a couple of hours later, I had in my mixer the most elastic dough with an incredible color. I had to adjust my baking—I changed my timing for mixing and started using autolysis—but I will never forget how wonderful the dough felt between my fingers on that first day.

The following day, after I removed my first loaves of "Orga bread" from the oven, I called Leif and this time he did not hang up on me. He went completely silent when I told him how fantastic his flour was and how ecstatic I was about the wonderful bread I had just baked. Thanks again, Leif, for bringing me the field in a sack. Great wheat, great flour, great baker, great bread. . . .

GREAT WHEAT

GREAT FLOUR

GREAT BAKER

GREAT BREAD

GREAT WHEAT

GREAT FLOUR

GREAT BAKER

GREAT BREAD

GREAT WHEAT

GREAT FLOUR

GREAT BAKER

GREAT BREAD

GREAT WHEAT

GREAT FLOUR

GREAT BAKER

GREAT BREAD

GREAT WHEAT

GREAT FLOUR

GREAT BAKER

GREAT BREAD

Located in the farmlands just outside Norrköping is the fantastic mill Orga. Brothers Lennart and Leif Nyman, fourth generation millers, manage the 150-year-old mill.

VETE MJÖL

2 KG NETTO

ETT MJÖL HELT UTAN TILLSATSER
från

ORGA KVARN
617 31 SKÄRBLACKA

La famille.

You must know where you come from to know where you are going.

I come from a family of bakers. We lived so close to the bakery that you could tell from anywhere in the house which breads or pastries were in the oven at any time. Our lives revolved around the bread, the cakes, and the croissants that we created almost every day—my parents' bakery was closed only one day a week, on Tuesdays, and during two weeks in July each year.

Every morning, I would come downstairs to get a croissant or a pain au chocolat from the bakery before I went to school. It was strictly forbidden to grab any of the finer samples, as they were intended for our customers. In the shop, everything was fast paced and rarely did anyone realize that I had snuck in there. My older brother worked in front of the big stone oven, shuffling baguettes in and out along with other larger breads while my father filled the store and our truck with sweet and savory breads fresh out of the oven. Later on, when the night baking came to an end, he would drive around to fifteen nearby villages where there were no bakeries, honking his car horn as he drove through the streets in the middle of the night.

At 5:30 a.m., my mother and my sister-in-law would have the store operating in full swing. They made sandwiches for the bakery's first morning customers. It was so enthralling to watch how they would run around, moving almost as if in a dance. They all stepped in harmony and made sure not to tread on any toes.

On the weekends I helped with anything and everything in the bakery. I loved to be there, and I completed all the boring tasks as quickly as possible—such as scraping plates, cleaning dishes, and greasing brioche pans—to make sure I had time to roll a couple of croissants or top some tarts with strawberries. It was very much a hierarchical world and my dad ran the place with clear rules; not just anyone could do anything. He would never consider allowing a first-year apprentice to decorate a mousse cake or score his large miche au levain. I was the exception to the rule, and even though I was the youngest one in the bakery, he let me try everything.

Sometimes he got large orders of chaussons aux pommes and he would then wake me up in the middle of the night to help him glaze them. It is extremely important for chaussons to be glazed as soon as they come out of the oven—they must be really hot when they get their sugar glaze, otherwise they will be ruined, sticky, and without any shine to them. So there I would be, in my pajamas with brush in hand, just wishing for it all to be finished so I could go back to sleep again. Dad was trying to make me pay attention to how beautiful all of this was, with the pans all lined

27

up next to each other, and how fantastic it was when the glaze touched the pans, how the apple pastries were singing *pppp-ccccc-chhhhiiiiitttt* to us. All I wanted to do was to get back into my bed, as I was too young to understand what he found so fascinating about puff pastry filled with apple compote.

It was always a dilemma for him to show me how beautiful his profession was, because he knew that there were many other professions that were not as strenuous on an everyday basis. My mother had made up her mind, and she worried that he would drag me into the bakery business as well.

Sometimes my mother would come into the bakery while my dad was showing me something interesting and in those moments she would look at him angrily and Dad would immediately put a stop to what we were doing.

I will never forget her look of terror the day I told her that I wanted to quit school to become a pastry chef. Despite her protests, I went my own way and I have never regretted my decision. I think my parents are proud today that I found happiness in creating large sourdough breads and baking them in a large stone oven.

They were so proud the day they came to my newly opened Stockholm bakery, Petite France, on a Saturday. The place was packed with guests and the line of customers extended all the way out to the sidewalk. People waited in line to buy my sourdough bread and my brother Damien's lovely pastries, as well as his wonderful macaroons.

Mom, Dad, the cat Chamallow, and the dove La Tourte, which had decided on its own to move in with us. She flew in and out of the house as she pleased.

28

My mother Arlette, at the age of four, with the family dog Youki.

à l'attaque!

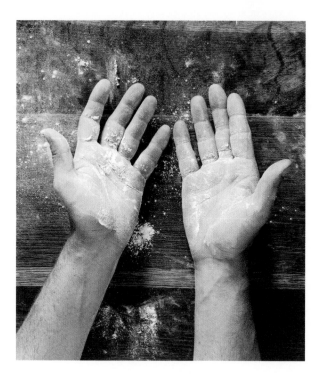

Everyone is different and we all think differently. This is also how it works when it comes to baking equipment. Of course it's nice to have tools that can help you achieve great results, but it's easy to get fooled into thinking that the quality of the bread depends on a bunch of equipment.

A large selection of equipment available on the market today are polished factory items marketed toward the home baker. A great example of this is the perforated baguette pan, which can, unfortunately, be found in most homes today. These pans allow the baguettes to turn out nice and round with pretty designs on the bottom—just like at 7-Eleven or similar stores that offer "bake-off baguettes." I've created some of my best breads without any fancy equipment whatsoever. An old plastic bowl, a linen towel with holes in it, a barely functioning gas oven, and, of course, my two hands, are all the tools I need.

There are, however, some tools I do recommend and they will make your sourdough bread smoother, better tasting, and more successful.

BAKING STONE Preserves and spreads the heat in the oven to give the bread a better crust. Great for baking right on top of the stone.

Tip! Turn the oven on at least one hour before you are going to bake to make sure the stone is completely hot.

PLASTIC CONTAINER The best and most even place for leavening is in a plastic container in the fridge. Here the temperature stays steady at 39–43°F (4–6°C) all year round. Buy two containers of different sizes (one must fit comfortably inside the other). Then place your dough (after it has started developing) into the smaller container. Then, put the small container into the larger container, like a Russian Matryoshka doll. This way, you create a great atmosphere for your dough and protect it from the air.

LEAVENING BASKET Preferably made from rattan and dressed with linen. The basket helps the bread rise and the linen fabric gives an indication as to when the bread has finished leavening. When the dough releases from the fabric and is no longer sticky, it has finished leavening.

Tip! Don't wait too long to bake the bread after you've removed the dough from the basket. You should put the loaf in the oven as soon as you remove it from the basket for maximum height.

BAKING TOWEL Preferably made from linen. The baking towel is used to cover the dough while it is resting or leavening to protect it from the air and prevent it from drying out. It's also used for separating baguettes, which otherwise have a tendency to stick together during the leavening process.

Tip! Never wash a baking towel made from linen. If mold starts to grow on it, put it in the oven at 250°F (120°C) for thirty minutes and brush the mold off afterward.

SCORING KNIFE Allows you to sign your creations. Scoring is extremely important as it helps your bread expand during the baking process and also makes it look prettier.

Tip! Bread that has not fully leavened needs deep scoring, while bread that has leavened for too long needs shallow scoring.

BREAD PEEL Prevents you from getting burned, plus the peel makes it easier to bake right on the baking stone.

Tip! Choose a bread peel that is as wide as your oven.

33

BAKING SOURDOUGH STEP BY STEP

When baking with sourdough, the most important thing of all is that you enjoy the moment and that you are proud of your accomplishment when you take the bread out of the oven. There is nothing in life that is objectively perfect; perfection has many faces and what is perfect for me might not be perfect for you. But there are a couple of golden rules and, if we respect them, we are more likely to succeed. Let's take it step by step.

paths

If you don't have a solid foundation, it is difficult to build a solid construction. Proportion is key if you want to bake bread with nice consistency and great taste. This is why I always measure my ingredients in weight instead of volume.

The volume of flour can differentiate itself significantly depending on several factors: if the flour bag has been on the top or the bottom of the shelf, how much air is in the bag, the temperature of the flour, and even when it was harvested. If you convert 1 cup of flour to ounces, the conversion difference can be between 1 to 2 ounces, and if you are supposed to add several cups, the proportions will end up off by quite a bit. I have included the standard conversions in each recipe; however, if you'd like to be as exact as possible, use the weight measured in grams (listed in parentheses for most ingredients). There is also a conversion table at the back of this book that offers the standard conversions for common ingredients.

Measuring by weight offers more precision and increases your chances of success in baking. And it will not cost you too much to buy a food scale, as they're not that expensive. Many people raise their eyebrows when I mention eggs in weight instead of numbers—but the weight of an egg can also vary by ounces, which can turn out to be a complete disaster if you are making brioche, for example. Even if I think it's important to weigh eggs, my recipes do have the number of eggs clearly defined in parentheses within them. These are meant as guidelines so you know if you have enough eggs at home or if you have to buy more before you begin baking.

Once you've weighed your ingredients, it is time to prepare the mix. The temperature of the dough after mixing should be 70–80°F (22–25°C). When preparing the dough, the water and flour should each be 70–80°F (22–25°C).

mixing

I think we all benefit from being in touch with our ingredients. The connection between the person and the dough heightens the enjoyment, and you create a relationship with the dough that is to become your bread. I love to mix by hand—it is like meditation for me and I recommend that everyone try it at least a few times. Mixing by hand gives you a feeling for the dough, and I think that it is difficult to truly understand how the dough works without having done so.

When I mix my dough, I prefer to use something that I call the la-fontaine method. The la-fontaine method consists of pouring the flour on the baking table; then I make a dent in the middle of the flour, into which I pour sourdough, liquids, and salt. I then work my way from the outside in by using a small amount of flour at a time.

1. Shape the flour into a circle and make a dent in the middle. Pour the sourdough in the dent.

2. Add water and salt to the dent.

3. Work the flour into the mix, a small amount at a time, as the walls of flour get thinner and thinner.

4. When you have worked all the flour into the mix, use a pastry scraper to assist you.

autolysis

Dough is never ready to be kneaded right after the mixing, and this is when time is your best friend.

It takes a little bit of time before each small flour particle absorbs the liquid; this is when the autolysis sets in. Autolysis is a resting element, which allows the proteins to absorb the optimal amount of liquid. This stage prepares the creation of the so-called gluten web, which makes the dough elastic before the kneading.

Right after the mixing, dough lacks structure—if you try to pull on the dough, it will usually fall apart at this point. But if you allow the dough to rest for forty-five minutes to an hour, the flour will have had enough time to absorb the liquid and the gluten net will have had enough time to develop. This process happens naturally, and after an hour, the dough stays in one piece without you having to do anything at all.

It is important to not mistake the fermentation for the autolysis. The dough is not supposed to leaven during autolysis, but instead lets the proteins prepare themselves for all the kneading. With the help of autolysis, you can begin baking real, robust bread using flour with lower protein levels. This way you can stay away from lesser quality flours that have plenty of additives. The dough also absorbs more liquid right from the start so you will have bread that is more moist in the end.

It is practically impossible to fail with autolysis and the only challenge you might have is figuring out what to do during the hour you are waiting for it to complete. Perhaps a glass of Burgundy and a couple of olives to pass the time?

kneading

For the same reason I recommend mixing with your hands, I recommend you knead with your hands every now and then. When you work with your hands, you get a real feel and understanding for how you want the dough mixer to work.

If you knead with your hands, the coarse sea salt will work as a timer to tell you when the dough is ready. When you no longer feel the grains of salt, the dough is ready. If you use a dough mixer, you will have to follow strict time lines. Kneading times can vary depending on dough, technique, and power. Keep in mind that dough made of natural flour without any additives is more sensitive and requires less kneading.

When the dough is smooth and releases from the table on its own and you can no longer feel any salt, it is ready. This can take five to fifteen minutes.

Give the dough an initial shape by making a round ball. Then let it rest, covered by a moist baking towel or in a plastic container with a lid, for two to five hours before you starting shaping it again.

shaping

To create beautiful bread, it is important to take your time when shaping it. If you shape the bread nicely—and, if possible, do it a couple of times, allowing it to rest in between—you will get a bread with nice height and volume.

When you shape the bread, it is important to first establish the top and the bottom of the loaf. When this is done, it is important to work consistently within these guidelines.

Grab hold of the shape from the bottom and fold it toward the middle of the top; the dough is supposed to be pulled from the bottom upward. Press down on top and repeat the procedure until you have a loaf with nice surface tension. When you are done shaping the loaf, you can test the surface tension by pressing a finger into the dough—if the dough has enough tension, it will immediately rise up again.

flouring

Sprinkle with flour frequently! Properly sprinkling flour on the dough one last time before leavening will ensure the dough retains more water, thus creating a nice and moist bread in the end. The flour will absorb the water that would otherwise evaporate during the leavening process.

The sprinkling of flour serves more than one function, however. When you bake the bread in the oven, the flour will also prevent the crust from developing too quickly. This allows the heat to reach the core of the bread more effectively, causing the bread to expand. The end result is a better crust.

ZZZ

Any resting time that occurs before the bread has been shaped is called downtime, and the resting time after shaping is what is known as leavening. When the bread has been shaped, it is now ready for leavening—preferably in a baking basket made from natural materials and lined at the bottom with linen fabric. The basket supports the bread and helps it rise upward. Since the basket is porous and allows the dough to breathe, the crust will also begin to develop during the leavening process.

Leavening of bread in the fridge does not necessarily mean that the dough is leavening cold. Bread that is leavening is actually "sweating" and producing heat; this is why bread rises best in a sealed and moist environment. Sometimes it can actually leaven too fast, so to prevent this from

happening, I usually put the dough in a basket, which I place in a smaller container and then put in a larger container—just like a Matryoshka doll.

Start the leavening at room temperature. Then put the dough in the containers and place them in the fridge overnight. When leavening in this way, you control the process, lowering the temperature gradually. Long and careful leavening gives the bread a better taste, and the phytic acid will have enough time to break down so the nutrients can be released within the bread.

When the bread has finished baking, it should have doubled in size. Half of the volume change should stem from the leavening and the rest of the increased volume should happen during scoring and baking.

scoring

Offering guests bread that has not been scored is like giving away flowers that will never bloom. Scored bread is like an open rose; it invites you in and reveals your signature to the world. But the scoring also serves a practical purpose—it gives you control. You score your bread so that it can burst open; scoring also helps the bread expand during baking. It's also a great way to fix bread that has leavened for too long or for too short a period of time. If you score bread a little deeper when it has not leavened to your expectations, you can make it rise enough to be perfect after all.

I recommend all enthusiastic bakers buy a scoring knife. You can use a regular knife, but since it's not as sharp as a proper scoring knife, your task will become more difficult. Alternately, you could use a razor blade attached to a small stick.

47

baking

It's easy to forget how important timing is when baking bread in the oven. However, what amounts to the final sentence at the end of a recipe is just as important as the recipe as a whole. This is why it's important for you to get to know your oven and to make sure you adjust all baking advice based on your own experiences.

Many home ovens have a limited capacity, but there are two things you can do, no matter what oven you have, to control the baking results. The first is to use a baking stone when you bake bread, and the second is to add moisture to your oven.

In a regular oven, the temperature drops drastically when you open the door, which means that the oven has to work hard to get the temperature up again after it has been closed. By using a baking stone, you can get around this. The stone retains the heat and distributes it more effectively, so you can avoid the drastic temperature drop when you put the bread in the oven. The stone should be placed on a guard or grate in the oven from the beginning. You then place your bread on the stone to bake. Make sure the stone you choose is approved for kitchen use and does not contain lead or other dangerous materials.

By throwing water into the oven or placing an oven pan or pot filled with hot water on the bottom of the oven, you create a moist environment, which protects the crust from getting hard and drying too fast during baking. This way, the heat in the oven has time to reach all the air bubbles inside the bread, allowing them to expand fully and making the bread light and airy.

A moist baking environment also prevents water inside the bread from evaporating, allowing the bread to retain more moisture.

If you choose to throw water in the oven, the water should be as close to boiling as possible. The idea is for steam to condense on the bread. Without steam, you will end up with a dull crust, which will prevent the bread from bursting and will increase the risk of dry bread.

Many suggest that warm air is the way to go when baking certain items and that only bottom heat should be used for other items, but I prefer the air in my oven to be still during baking. I don't want to ruin the peace and harmony in my oven with rotating air. I never open the oven door during baking because I don't want to let out any of the steam. I believe in preserving a nice balance of heat and moisture in the oven all the way until the baking is complete.

The baking element is fascinating. It brings to life my visions of creating bread from dough, making sugar caramelize, and creating tarts from puff pastry. For me, the oven is the heart that beats and spreads its warmth throughout the whole bakery.

49

patience

If you cut the bread too soon after removing it from the oven, all your hard work will have been for naught. Unfortunately, the resting element—*le ressuage*—is a very important process that many ignore. When you cut into the bread too early, I imagine the bread is "bleeding." The moisture, which is still in the form of steam at this point, needs time to condense, and if you give the bread the time to do so it will taste better, last longer, and will have a better crust. However, if you cut into the bread too early, it will lose its flavor and become soggy. Let the bread rest until it has an inner temperature of less than 100°F (40°C)—it only takes about thirty minutes to an hour, depending on the size of the loaf. Never place the bread directly onto the kitchen counter—let it cool down on a rack so it can breathe. Nor should you cover it with a baking towel; when you do so, you prohibit the bread from creating its crust.

It is a good idea to keep the cooled bread in a paper bag or wrapped up in cloth. I prefer to keep it standing up on its edge after I have tasted my first slice, with the cut end toward the counter. I will then cover it with a baking towel.

50

SOURDOUGH BREAD

Bread is life. It is my life and my way of telling my story. Perhaps it sounds a little strange that with flour, water, and salt, you can tell a story about yourself or tell your family and friends that you love them. But no matter what recipe you follow, you are the one that ends up reflected in the bread you pull from the oven. A recipe is just a support system, a well of inspiration, that disappears as your bread takes its shape. My wish and hope is that you—the person who is baking bread following the recipes in this book— forget about both me and the recipe as you cut that first piece of the bread you made. Because in that moment, the bread is yours—your expression.

STARTING A SOURDOUGH

Baking sourdough bread is easy, but first you need a sourdough starter. This starter will ensure that your sourdough will leaven later. A sourdough starter can be stored at room temperature for as long as you want, so long as it gets fed once or twice a week. Remember, all volumes are meant as indications only. Every sourdough is unique and the absorption ability of flour varies depending on season of year and kind (rye flour, for example, needs more water than wheat). Feel free to use two or three kinds of flour in your sourdough to increase the chance of a successful bacterial culture. I recommend that you use flour without additives. As I have previously mentioned, additives are not dangerous or bad for sourdough, but you will most likely end up with flour that is sterile.

DAY 1

You will need: A glass jar with a lid that can hold about 2 cups (500 ml) + fork + water + rye flour + wheat flour.

Pour ⅓ cup (100 ml) tepid water into a clean jar. (Instead of using dish detergent to clean it, place the jar in a warm oven for a few minutes.) Add ¼ cup (50 ml) flour and ¼ cup (50 ml) rye flour. Stir with a fork until you get a smooth, slow-moving batter. The water and flour quantities do not have to be exact; the important thing is that you achieve a consistency similar to pancake batter. Store the sourdough starter at room temperature with the lid slightly ajar so the air can reach the starter. A good practice is to cover the jar with an upside down plastic bowl.

DAY 2

There should now be air bubbles in the sourdough and you ought to be able to detect a mild and aromatic scent. Don't worry if the sourdough has not yet started to develop, as the process can take up to two days depending on the temperature of the room and the kind of flour you use. Feed the sourdough with ½ cup (100 ml) water, ¼ cup (50 ml) rye flour, and ¼ cup (50 ml) wheat flour and stir. Store at room temperature with the lid ajar and preferably with an upside down plastic bowl covering it.

DAY 3

Feed the sourdough with ½ cup (100 ml) water, ¼ cup (50 ml) rye flour, and ¼ cup (50 ml) wheat flour. Stir and store at room temperature with the lid ajar.

DAY 4

Hopefully by now, the sourdough is ready for baking. For each day you feed your sourdough, the time it takes for the sourdough to bubble decreases. A fresh and ripe sourdough usually starts to bubble two to five hours after feeding. Test it by shaking or tilting the jar carefully; you will notice that it moves almost on its own. There is life in there, and now it is time for you to make sourdough bread out of it.

Please note: Don't forget to feed your sourdough starter the day before you intend to bake with it. However, don't feed it right after you have baked with it if you are not planning to bake again the following day.

55

THE LEVAIN FAMILY

There are different ways to bake sourdough bread. The floating sourdough is what is traditionally called sourdough, while the levain method is a leavening method that uses solid sourdough. There are many misconceptions surrounding the true meaning of levain. Some people believe that it is a certain kind of bread that looks a certain kind of way. Wrong! Levain is not a type of bread; it is a method of leavening. Bread baked with the levain method can be dark or white, slim or thick. You can make pizza dough, ciabatta, and cinnamon rolls using levain.

Let's start from the beginning. Levain, as a leavening method, is based on mixing part of a fermented dough with a new dough, so that the new dough will be affected by the power of the yeast. When you bake with the levain method, you don't use the entire dough. Instead, you save a small part, which will be the starter for the next dough. All batches of dough are linked together like siblings and they work in tandem with each other. To feed dough with a piece of levain is like planting a seed in the soil—a chain reaction will take place and will create life once more in the new dough. People have been baking with the levain method since the Middle Ages. Today, it is a method used mostly by bakers and those who bake bread every day. The difference between floating sourdough and levain is more philosophical than culinary, though there are some differences in flavor. The levain method can be compared to a marathon runner who is able to run for a longer period of time, while the floating sourdough is more like a short distance runner. Both methods have pros and cons. Floating sourdough is suitable for the home baker since it does not require baking every day. Levain, on the other hand, will die if you don't bake with it at least every other day.

This is how you create *levain chef* at home:

DAY 1
Mix together ¼ cup (50 g) floating sourdough, ¾ cup (75 g) finely stone-ground rye flour, and ½ cup (125 g) tepid water. Store in a plastic or glass jar with a lid.

DAY 2 AND DAY 3
Feed the sourdough with ¾ cup (75 g) finely stone-ground rye flour and ½ cup (125 g) tepid water.

DAY 4
Feed the sourdough with ¾ cup (75 g) finely stone-ground rye flour.

DAY 5
Mix 2 cups (500 g) cold water, 3 cups (300 g) finely stone-ground rye flour, 3½ cups (450 g) wheat flour, 1½ cup (300 g) floating sourdough (the result of the above-made sourdough) in a large bowl. Stir with a wooden spoon until your dough sticks together. Let the dough rest for thirty minutes. Shape the dough into a round loaf and put it back in the bowl. Cover the dough with a baking towel and let it leaven at room temperature for twelve hours or until doubled in size. From now on, you can replace your floating sourdough with a piece of levain. Save a piece from each time you bake and use it to leaven the next time.

You should use between 7 and 14 ounces (200 and 400 g) of levain dough per quart (liter) of water.

COMMON SOURDOUGH QUESTIONS

HOW DO I STORE A SOURDOUGH STARTER?

Cold temperatures can make your sourdough really sour and, for that reason, I always store my sourdough starter at room temperature—never in the fridge. Storing the sourdough starter at room temperature will give the bread a rounder flavor that is gentle and mild. However, if you are baking Finnish sourdough rye bread, you should definitely store it in the fridge. But for all recipes in this book, I recommend storing the sourdough at room temperature.

HOW OFTEN SHOULD I FEED THE SOURDOUGH?

Feed your sourdough starter the day before you are going to bake with it. If you are not baking for a few weeks—or months—it is enough to feed it once or twice a week. Throw away 75 percent of the sourdough starter and then feed it according to the same principle as before: ⅓ cup water and ½ cup flour of your choice without additives.

CAN A SOURDOUGH STARTER DIE?

Probably not. Most sourdough starters can be revived.

IS THERE A RISK OF OVERFEEDING THE SOURDOUGH?

If you feed the sourdough before it has begun to bubble again from the last feeding, there is a chance that it will not bubble again. Have patience and give your sourdough starter the time it needs.

SOURDOUGH TIPS

• "Bake" the glass jar you use to store your sourdough in the oven instead of washing it. Sourdough is a culture of microorganisms that are sensitive to pressure, temperature changes, and chemicals (such as dish detergent, which might be left in there if you don't rinse it properly). This is why I recommend baking the jar in the oven to sterilize.

• Sourdough starters prefer warmth, moisture, and air. Find a place in the kitchen where the temperature stays the same (but not above 110°F/45°C). Avoid keeping it close to the stove, where temperatures can fluctuate between hot and cold.

• Always start off a sourdough starter with flour of good quality, preferably organic and definitely free of additives.

• Try mixing several kinds of flour and try using stone-ground flour for an increased chance at creating a live bacterial culture.

• If the sourdough starter is beginning to break, add more flour and stir.

• Always feed the sourdough starter the day before you bake with it.

PAVÉ

Pavé is my signature bread and it represents who I am as a baker and as a person. Thanks to its prolonged leavening, perfect pavé has time to develop deep and complex flavors. It is intricate but still very simple in taste, with a nice chewy resistance that melts in your mouth. Behind its thick crust you will find a creamy interior. Pavé was, in earlier times, pretty tall and square in shape, hence the name (pavé = pavement). But in time, I came to think that its shape was not in harmony with its flavor. A round flavor for a square-shaped bread . . . No, the pavé needed a new dress—and I chose an asymmetrical score and shape, which when cut in two, creates two unique shapes.

1 LOAF

4 cups (500 g) stone-ground wheat flour
2½ cups (250 g) stone-ground rye flour
2 cups (500 g) tepid water
3 tsp (20 g) unrefined coarse sea salt
1 cup (200 g) floating sourdough
or 1 cup (200 g) levain dough

DAY 1

1. Mix wheat and rye flour on a baking table and create a dent in the middle. Add water, salt, and sourdough to the dent. Work the ingredients into the flour a little at a time until the dough is solid. Add more flour if the dough feels too soft.
2. Let the dough go through autolysis by letting it rest under a baking towel for an hour. (Learn more about autolysis on page 41.)
3. Knead the dough for about another 15 minutes by hand or for about 10 minutes in a dough mixer on the lowest speed.
4. Let the dough rest on the table for 10 minutes.
5. Fold the dough in half. Sprinkle flour on top and put it in a plastic container with a baking towel on the bottom and a lid on top. Let the dough rest at room temperature for 1–2 hours so it can begin to develop. Then store the container in the fridge for 24 hours.

DAY 2

After 24 hours, the dough should have doubled in size. If it has not, you can let the container stand at room temperature with the lid on for a few hours.

1. Pour the dough onto a bed of flour on a baking table and shape it carefully into a loaf, moving the dough toward your body.
2. Return the pavé to the plastic container and sprinkle plenty of flour on top. Place the lid on the container and put it back in the fridge for another 24 hours.

DAY 3

1. Preheat the oven to 500°F (260°C).
2. Pour the dough onto a bread peel or directly onto parchment paper. Sprinkle flour on the dough and score the pavé with a scoring knife or razor.
3. Lower the oven temperature to 450°F (240°C) and throw boiling hot water onto the bottom of the oven to create steam. Bake the bread for 50 minutes in the middle of the oven.
4. Remove the bread from the oven and let it cool on a rack for at least 45 minutes.

LE PAIN AU LEVAIN

Le pain au levain—the original legend! A bread with a rich, ancient history that is something of a rarity, since the knowledge behind this marvelous bread has disappeared and today's flour has become more and more sterile. Levain bread demands flour of high quality—organic and stone-ground flour offer the best results. Real levain does not have any yeast in it—that's the whole point of the bread.

1 LOAF

4 cups (500 g) wheat flour
1¼ cups (125 g) rye flour
1¼ cups (125 g) durum wheat
2 cups (500 g or ½ liter) tepid water
3 tsp (20 g) unrefined coarse sea salt
1½ cups (300 g) levain dough

DAY 1

1. Mix wheat, rye, and durum flour on a baking table and make a dent in the middle. Add water and salt to the dent and work the flour into the liquid—a little at a time—until you have dough that is soft and quite sticky. Let the dough rest under a baking towel for 1 hour.

2. Knead the dough for 10 minutes by hand or for 7 minutes in a dough mixer at the lowest speed. Add the levain dough and knead for another 5 minutes by hand or for 3 minutes in the mixer.

3. Let the dough rest for 2 hours covered by a moist baking towel.

4. Shape the dough into a round loaf. Sprinkle flour on top and let it rest for 20 minutes at room temperature.

5. Shape it and sprinkle with flour one more time. Place the dough upside down in a leavening basket that has also been sprinkled with flour. Place the basket in a plastic container with a lid. Place the container in the fridge and let the bread leaven for 12 to 24 hours.

DAY 2

1. Preheat the oven to 500°F (260°C).

2. Pour the dough onto a baking peel or directly onto parchment paper by turning the basket upside down. Sprinkle the loaf with plenty of flour and score it with a razor or scoring knife.

3. Reduce the heat to 450°F (240°C) and throw some boiling hot water onto the bottom of the oven to create steam. Bake the bread for 50 minutes in the oven.

4. Remove the bread from the oven and let it cool on a rack for at least 45 minutes.

65

DURUM PAVÉ

This is a variation of my signature bread—the pavé. The method is the same as in the original, but I use durum wheat instead of stone-ground rye flour. Durum wheat flour contains much more protein and the result is a crunchier crust and a more intensely yellow interior.

1 LOAF

4 cups (500 g) stone-ground wheat flour
2½ cups (250 g) durum wheat flour
2 cups (500 g/500 ml) tepid water
3 tsp unrefined coarse sea salt
½–1 cup (100–200 g) floating sourdough
or ½–1 cup (100–200 g) levain dough

DAY 1

1. Mix wheat and durum flour on a baking table and make a dent in the middle. Add water, salt, and sourdough to the dent. Work the ingredients into the flour, a little at a time, until your dough is solid. Add more flour if the dough feels too soft. Let the dough rest at room temperature under a baking towel for 1 hour.
2. Knead the dough for about 10–15 minutes by hand or for 10 minutes in a dough mixer on the lowest speed.
3. Sprinkle the dough with flour and let it rest for 10 minutes at room temperature.
4. Fold the dough in half. Sprinkle flour on top and put it in a plastic container with a baking towel on the bottom and a sealing lid on top. Store in the fridge for 24 hours.

DAY 2

After 24 hours, the dough should have doubled in size. If it hasn't, you can let the container stand at room temperature with the lid on for a few hours.

1. Pour the dough onto a bed of flour on a baking table and carefully shape into a loaf. Make sure to shape the dough toward your body.
2. Return the dough to the plastic container and sprinkle plenty of flour on top. Place the lid on the container and put it back in the fridge for another 24 hours.

DAY 3

1. Preheat the oven to 500°F (260°C).
2. Pour the dough onto a bread peel or directly onto parchment paper. Sprinkle flour onto the dough and score the bread with a razor or a scoring knife.
3. Reduce the oven temperature to 450°F (240°C) and throw boiling hot water onto the bottom of the oven to create steam. Bake the bread for 50 minutes in the middle of the oven.
4. Remove the bread from the oven and let it cool on a rack for at least 45 minutes.

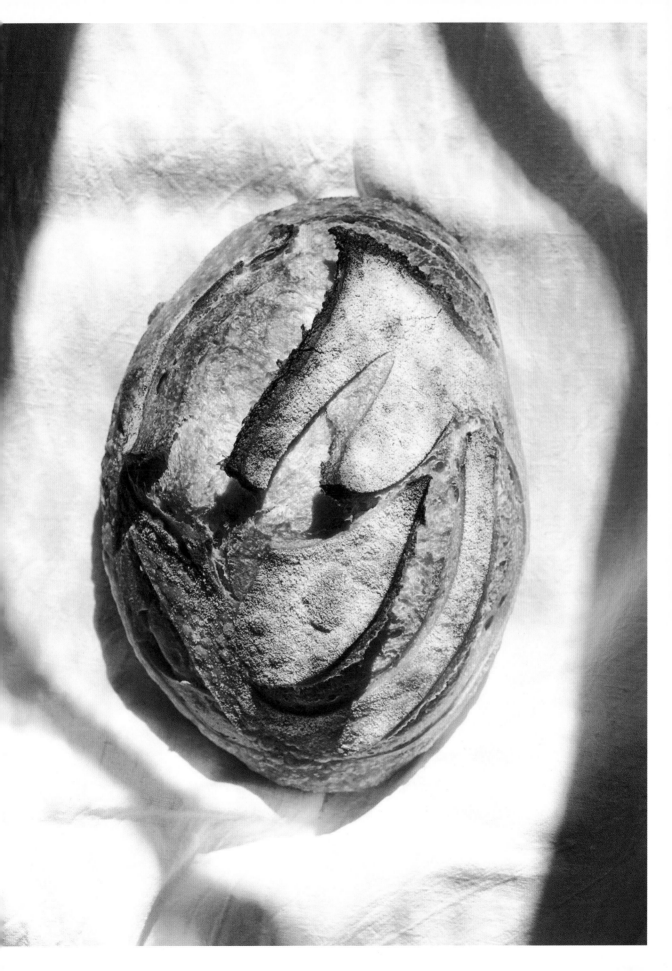

BEETROOT BREAD WITH CHÈVRE

Is it bread or a complete meal? This bread has everything. Roast the beetroots on a bed of sea salt and save the salt for the next time you boil potatoes—it will give them a nice pink color.

1 LOAF

1 batch durum pavé up until day 1, step 4
  (pg. 66)
2 cups (260 g) beetroots
2¼ cups (650 g) coarse sea salt for roasting
9½ oz (260 g) chèvre cheese
1 stem rosemary
a large pinch of fleur de sel (fine sea salt)
a large pinch of freshly ground black pepper

DAY 1

1. Prepare the durum pavé up until step 4.
2. Pour coarse sea salt on a baking sheet and spread out the beetroots. Roast the beetroots in the oven at 285–425°F (140–220°C) until they cook completely—poke them with a stick to make sure they're fully roasted. Let the beetroots rest at room temperature until the following day.

DAY 2

1. Remove the dough container from the fridge and let it stand at room temperature for 20 minutes.
2. In the meantime, peel the beetroots. (If you don't want the world to know for the next week that you've been roasting beetroots, make sure to wear plastic gloves—just be careful, as they have a tendency to slip easily.) Cut the beetroots into large pieces and make sure they have enough salt on them.
3. Pour the dough onto a baking table and stretch it as far as you can without it breaking. Spread out half the beetroots over the dough and fold it in half. Spread out the rest of the beetroots on top of the dough and fold it in half once more.

4. Sprinkle flour on top of the dough and put it in a plastic container with flour on the bottom and a tightly sealed lid on top. Let it leaven for a few hours at room temperature before you put it in the refrigerator to leaven for another 12 to 24 hours.

DAY 3

After 24 hours, the dough should have doubled in size. If it has not, let the container with the dough stand at room temperature with the lid on for a few hours.

1. Preheat the oven to 475°F (250°C).
2. Carefully lift the dough from the container and put it upside down on a floured baking peel or on a baking sheet covered with parchment paper.
3. Cut the chèvre into quarters. Press down a piece of chèvre in the middle of one half of the dough. Take one of the corners of the dough and fold it toward the middle so that the chèvre is covered. Press down another piece of chèvre and fold in the next corner so it is completely covered. Repeat until all four corners are folded.
4. Stick a rosemary stem into the dough to hold it together; this will prevent the bread from opening like a flower during baking. If the dough has deflated during this procedure, you can cover it with a baking towel and let it leaven for few more hours.
5. Sprinkle flour on top of the dough and score. Sprinkle a pinch of fleur de sel and black pepper on top.
6. Reduce the temperature of the oven to 450°F (240°C) and bake the bread in the middle of the oven for 45–55 minutes.
7. Let the bread rest on a rack.

69

Always roast nuts before you add them to dough.

Figs poached in red wine add a wonderful flavor to bread. See recipe on page 77.

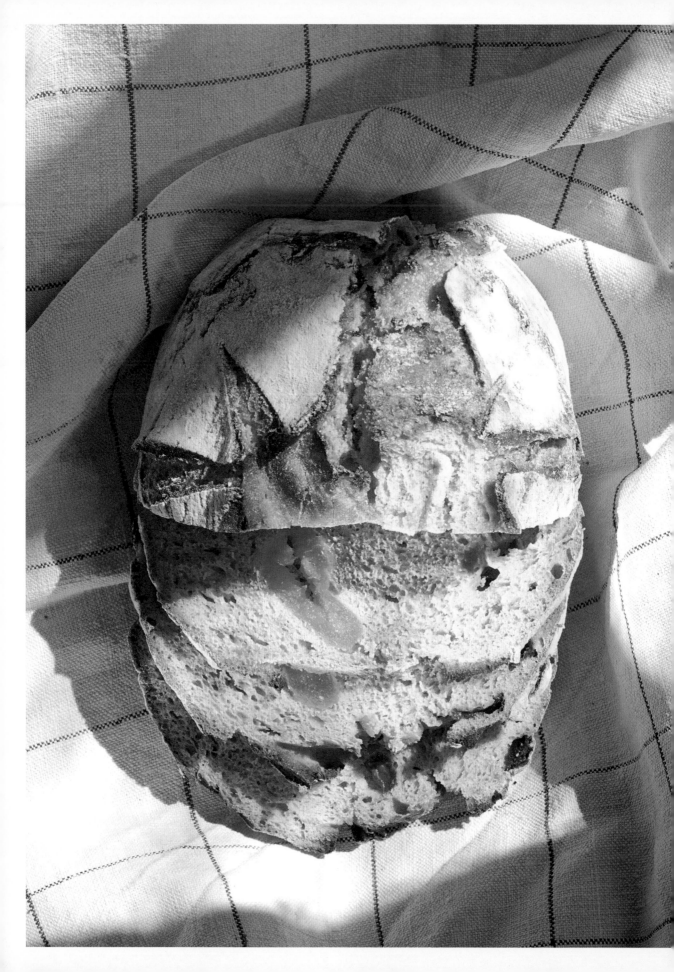

FRUIT BREAD

Figs, sultanas, cherries, apricots, goji berries, dates, or cranberries . . . Almost all dried fruits and berries are good to bake with. The secret behind a really moist fruit bread is to return the moisture to the dried fruit the right way. With too much water, they become too soft and mushy; with too little water, the fruit absorbs the moisture from the bread and this dries it out.

1 LOAF
1 batch pavé up until step 4 (pg. 63)
3¾ cups (450 g) sun-dried fruit
   (for example: figs, raisins, or apricots)
4 cups (1000 g/1 liter) cold water

DAY 1

1. Prepare the pavé up until step 4. Place the dough in a plastic container with a baking towel on the bottom, covered with flour, and a tightly sealed lid on top. Let the dough rest in the fridge overnight.
2. Mix the fruit in a bowl (if you use figs, make sure to cut off the ends first) and pour the water over them. Cover the bowl with plastic wrap. Let the fruit soak overnight at room temperature.

DAY 2

1. Drain the water from the fruit.
2. Depending on what you prefer, you can choose to add the fruit into the dough whole or you can mash them a little bit before adding. Whole pieces make for prettier bread while mashed fruit gives a better flavor. I usually do a combination of both, so it's both pretty and tasty.
3. Pour out the dough onto a baking table and stretch it as much as you can without breaking it. Spread out half the fruit on top of the dough and fold it in half. Spread out the rest of the fruit on top of the dough and fold the dough again. You can knead the dough a little to mash the fruit into it or if you want to keep it pretty, simply refrain from kneading at all.
4. Sprinkle flour on top of the dough and place it in a plastic container with a baking towel on the bottom and a tight sealing lid. Let the container with the dough rest at room temperature for about 1 hour or until the leavening process begins.
5. Place the container in the refrigerator and let the dough leaven for 12–24 hours.

DAY 3

After 12–24 hours in the refrigerator, the bread should have doubled in size. If it has not done so, simply leave out the container with the dough at room temperature for a few hours.

1. Carefully pour the dough onto a baking table and shape it into a square loaf. Place the loaf on a baking peel or on a baking sheet covered with parchment paper. Sprinkle a little bit of flour on top and let the loaf rest under a moist baking towel for 30 minutes.
2. Preheat the oven to 475°F (250°C).
3. Sprinkle the bread with flour and score it. Bake the bread for 30 minutes in the middle of the oven. Reduce the heat to 425°F (220°C) and bake for another 15 minutes.
4. Remove the bread from the oven and let it cool on a rack for at least 45 minutes.

WALNUT BREAD

Walnut bread has given me a taste for walnuts. But feel free to adjust the recipe by using pine nuts, hazelnuts, or almonds. I always roast the nuts first. Raw nuts don't have as much flavor as roasted nuts, and since the interior of the bread never reaches higher than 203–208°F (95–98°C), roasting is extremely important for enhancing the flavor.

1 LOAF
1 batch le pain au levain up until day 1,
step 2 (page 65)
2 cups (260 g) roasted walnuts

DAY 1
1. Prepare the levain up to step 2. Let the dough rest for 30 minutes.
2. Place the dough upside down on a baking table, sprinkled with flour, and stretch it as much as possible without breaking it.
3. Spread out half the walnuts on top of the dough and fold the dough in half. Spread out the rest of the nuts and fold the dough again.
4. Place the dough in a plastic container with a baking towel sprinkled with flour on the bottom and a tight sealing lid. Let the dough rest in the container for 2–3 hours at room temperature.
5. Remove the dough from the container and shape it into a nice oval-shaped loaf. Sprinkle flour on top and return the loaf to the container. Let it leaven in the fridge for 12–24 hours.

DAY 2
1. Preheat the oven to 475°F (250°C).
2. Pour the dough onto a baking peel or directly onto a baking sheet with parchment paper. Sprinkle flour on top and score the bread.
3. Bake the bread in the middle of the oven for about 45 minutes.

4. Remove the bread from the oven and let it cool on a rack for at least 45 minutes.

KEEP IN MIND . . .
• Always roast the nuts first—otherwise they will barely have any flavor.
• Nuts give color to the interior of the bread. This is why it's better to fold the nuts into the dough instead of pressing them into it.
• Nuts distribute oils to the dough and make the bread both easier to cut and chew.

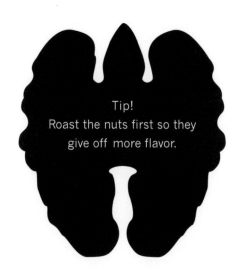

Tip!
Roast the nuts first so they give off more flavor.

74

RED WINE-POACHED FIG BREAD

This bread has a wonderful texture and is perfectly suited for pairing with dessert cheeses—especially goat cheese. Cut off the ends of the figs to make sure they can fully absorb the wine. Since the wine-poached figs are added before leavening, the bread will absorb this great flavor completely.

1 LOAF
1 batch pain au levain up until step 3
  (pg. 65)
32 sun-dried figs
1 bottle of red wine (750 ml)
12 bay leaves

DAY 1
1. Prepare the levain dough up until step 3.
2. Cut off the ends of the figs and place the figs in an oven or a copper pan. Pour the wine over the figs and add the bay leaves. Cut a piece of parchment paper to the size of the pan and place it on top of the figs so that the paper makes direct contact with the wine.
3. Preheat the oven to 175°F (80°C) and place the pan in the oven overnight *or* let the figs poach on the stove for 30 minutes.
4. Drain the wine from the figs and let the figs cool. (Save the wine in a plastic container and refrigerate. It's perfect for fruit salad in a red wine sauce or it can be used the next time you make this bread.)
5. Place the dough upside down on a baking table sprinkled with flour and stretch it as much as possible without breaking it. Spread half the figs out on top of the dough and fold the dough in half. Spread out the rest of the figs and fold the dough in half once more. Let the dough rest for 30 minutes at room temperature.
6. Shape the dough into a ball and place it in a plastic container with a baking towel sprinkled with flour on the bottom. Let the dough leaven at room temperature for a couple of hours. Place the container in the fridge and let the dough leaven for 12–24 hours.

DAY 2
The dough should now have doubled in size.

1. Preheat the oven to 475°F (250°C).
2. Carefully remove the dough from the container and shape it gently without removing any air bubbles. Place a bay leaf on top of the loaf, and put the bread on a baking sheet covered with parchment paper.
3. Bake the bread for 30 minutes in the middle of the oven. Then reduce heat to 425°F (220°C) and bake for another 20 minutes.
4. Remove the bread from the oven and let it cool on a rack for at least 45 minutes.

LA BAGUETTE

The baguette is the France's most popular and most purchased bread—and it's the worst of their selection of fine breads! The baguette you normally find in stores and bakeries is a fluffy white bread, without crust or color. But with the help of the poolish method, you can create beautiful and tasty baguettes. The Polish people brought this leavening method to France at the end of the 1800s, and it is based around letting three-fifths of the bread go through a prolonged autolysis (pg. 41) of twelve hours. The small amount of yeast creates a snowball effect, which begins the whole leavening process and produces airy bread with simple but clear sourdough flavor. This method is perfect for baking baguettes.

5 BAGUETTES

8 cups (1 kg) wheat flour + 5 cups (600 g)
　wheat flour
.03 oz (1 g) fresh yeast
4 cups (1000 g/1 liter) water
1½ oz (45 g) unrefined coarse sea salt

DAY 1

1. Prepare the poolish by whisking the 8 cups wheat flour, yeast, and water in a large bowl until you have the consistency of pancake batter.

2. Cover the bowl with a baking towel and let it leaven at room temperature for 12–16 hours.

DAY 2

After 12–16 hours of leavening, the dough should be doubled in size and will smell really nice.

1. Pour the 5 cups of wheat flour onto a baking table. Create a dent in the middle and pour the poolish from the previous day into the dent along with the sea salt. Mix and knead the dough (there is no need for autolysis since ⅗ of the dough has already rested for 12 hours with the water) until it releases from the table. Shape the dough into a ball and let it rest under a baking towel for 30 minutes.

2. Divide the dough into five equal parts and shape each one into a small ball. Let rest for a couple of minutes under a baking towel.

3. Carefully shape the balls into baguettes. If you notice that the dough begins to tear, you can let it rest a little bit longer so it can recover.

4. Sprinkle flour on the baking towel and place the first baguette on it. Fold the towel as in the picture to the right and place the next baguette alongside of the fold. Alternate between fold and baguette until the towel is covered—that way the baguettes won't touch each other but will still support one another.

5. Sprinkle flour on top of the baguettes and cover them with another baking towel. Let the baguettes leaven at room temperature for 3–4 hours or until doubled in size.

6. Preheat the oven to 500°F (260°C).

7. Remove them from the baking towel, score the flour-dusted baguettes lengthwise—carefully and not too quickly, as they can lose their structure. Note: Never score baguettes straight across.

8. Bake the baguettes in the middle of the oven for 20–25 minutes.

9. Let the baguettes cool down on a rack for at least 45 minutes.

78

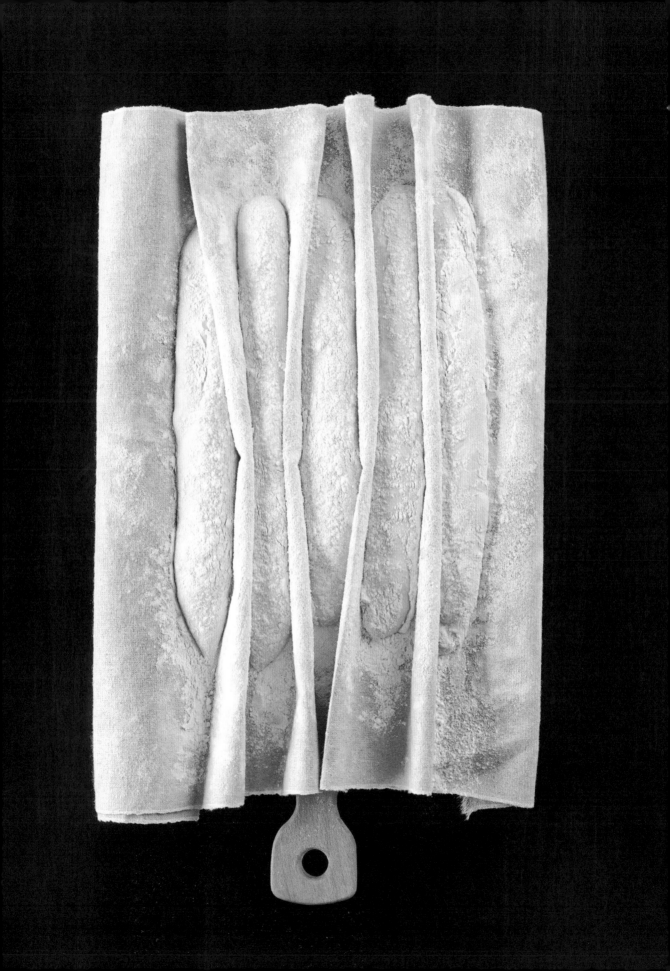

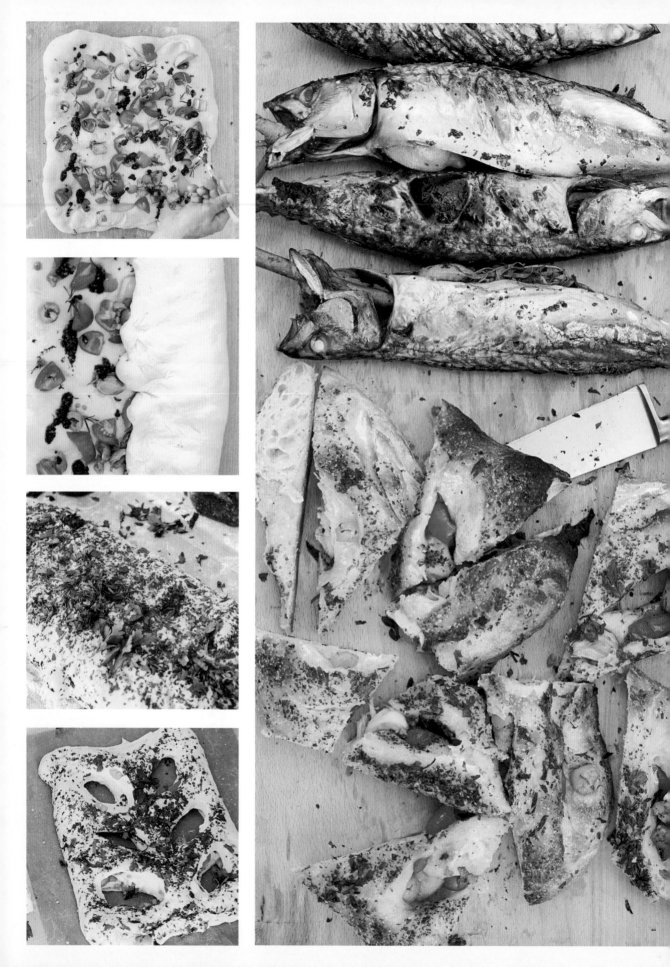

FOUGASSE

Fougasse represents sun, warmth, family, and friends to me. It's a perfect type of bread to eat at a barbeque or picnic. It's also almost impossible to make a mistake when baking it—fill the fougasse with the ingredients you love the most and nothing can go wrong. Serve the fougasse with a nice, cold rosé wine from Provence.

3 LOVELY FOUGASSE LOAVES
1 batch baguette dough, up until day 2,
   step 1 (pg. 78)
1 cored red pepper
1 cored yellow pepper
1 large, ripe, coarsely chopped tomato
1 head of garlic
1 handful chopped parsley
1 handful chopped thyme
a pinch of fleur de sel (fine sea salt)
¾ cup (180 g/200 ml) olive oil
freshly ground black pepper

DAY 1
1. Prepare the poolish for the baguette dough (pg. 78).

DAY 2
1. Continue preparing the dough up until step 1, day 2. Let the dough leaven for 2–3 hours at room temperature under a moist baking towel.
2. Roast the peppers and the head of garlic in the oven for a couple of minutes. Then let the peppers rest in ice water for a few minutes.
3. Peel the peppers and garlic. Cut the peppers into large chunks.

4. Mix the parsley, thyme, black pepper, salt, garlic, and vegetables in a bowl. Pour the olive oil on top of the mix.
5. Stretch the baguette dough as much as possible without breaking it. Spread the vegetable mix over the whole dough (gently drain the olive oil from it by pressing on the vegetables, and then save it for glazing the bread later).
6. Fold one of the long edges toward the middle (see picture on the left) and then repeat the step with the other side so the mix is completely covered. Cut the dough into three even pieces and let them rest for 1 hour under a moist baking towel.
7. Preheat the oven to 500°F (260°C).
8. Score the three dough pieces with the help of a pastry scraper. Stretch the dough gently to let the scores expand and create holes in the bread.
9. Glaze the bread with the oil from the vegetable mix and bake the first fougasse in the middle of the oven for about 25 minutes. Repeat the procedure for the other two fougasses.
10. Serve the bread while it is still warm, accompanied by a glass of cold rosé wine. Dip the fougasse in a small bowl of olive oil sprinkled with fleur de sel.

My great-grandmother and me at our farm.

Mom, dad, grandma, and great-grandma taking a break during the workday.

La Martelière.

My Childhood Paradise

La Martelière was the name of my parents' summer home—a rundown 150-year-old farm they bought when they were in their thirties. We spent the weekends there once a month and, of course, our holidays and vacations. I cannot describe how it felt to leave the hectic city of Paris and be absorbed by the luscious and quiet countryside of La Martelière. It was a simple farm without any running water, and I remember having to go out in the backyard to get water from the big cast-iron hand pump to brush my teeth. The water was ice cold and tasted like dirt and rust. As time went by, we slowly but surely renovated the farm so that we could come to stay during even the coldest of winter days. My parents had never been afraid of big changes, so one day they decided to sell our house in Paris. It was in June 1982 and I was just about to turn seven—a small boy from Paris moving to the country. We didn't have a lot of money, but vegetables were growing in our garden and outside the house there was a gigantic cherry tree that could produce more than 220 pounds (100 kg) of cherries on a good year. I knew that tree and each individual branch inside and out.

That tree was my second home. In time, we bought lots of animals and our home started to look more like the farm it once was. During all the years we lived there, we were essentially self-sufficient. I still remember how I disliked going down to the cellar to get a glass jar of green beans, a rillette, or a bottle of cider for dinner. Today, it's my dream to live like that! We baked bread once a week, and on certain Saturdays, we were treated to pain au chocolat. The biggest privilege of growing up in a family bakery was that we always had fresh bread on the table, no matter how poor we were. Bread is comfort. That is something I learned early on. Today, our La Martelière is gone. It was sold and has been completely updated into a soulless building with no remnant of its past. I remember the sadness I felt when I went by the house a few years ago with my children to show them a piece of my childhood. Everything was gone. The house had been turned into something unrecognizable and the giant cherry tree was no longer standing. But my memories live on and I am so glad and grateful that I had the privilege to grow up in a paradise like La Martelière.

SOS

Save Our Sourdough

Great quality sourdough bread begins with fresh, bubbling sourdough. There is no way around it. Trying to bake with sourdough when it is completely flat, broken, bad smelling, or moldy is just a waste of time and ingredients. I know that many recommend keeping the sourdough in the fridge, but I am convinced that it does best at room temperature. Cold temperatures make bread more sour and not as mild and aromatic in flavor as when you leave it at room temperature. The best way to keep sourdough at its finest is, of course, to bake with it often. But I understand that not everyone has the ability to do so. So let's go through the various stages of sourdough and talk about what can be done when common problems arise. Most problems happen when the sourdough has not been fed for a long period of time. If it has been longer than a week since you last fed the sourdough, it's best to throw away 75 percent of what is in the container and then to feed what's left with fresh water and flour.

WHAT DO I DO IF THE SOURDOUGH HAS BROKEN?

The sourdough usually breaks when it has not been fed for a while or if it is too loose in consistency. Add more flour and stir vigorously. If that doesn't work, throw away 75 percent of the sourdough and feed it again every couple of days.

THE SOURDOUGH DOESN'T BUBBLE EVEN THOUGH I HAVE FED IT

This can be due to several reasons:
• Check your flour bags. If they are old and have been open for a long time, you can try feeding your sourdough with flour from a fresh bag.
• Check the room temperature. If it is below 65°F (18°C) it will take longer for the sourdough to bubble. Throw away 75 percent of the sourdough in the container and feed it again, but this time use water that is a little bit warmer than before.
• The sourdough has turned too sour (pH-level is too low). Throw away 75 percent of the sourdough and feed it again with warmer water.

WHAT DO I DO IF THE SOURDOUGH IS MOLDY?

If the sourdough is beginning to grow mold, it's probably because it is not sour enough. I recommend that you throw all of it out and begin again.

P.S. Remember that a great and ripe sourdough that is ready for baking should already be bubbling 1–3 hours after you have fed it.

MUESLI

Sweet, great tasting, and so healthy! It magically transforms any yogurt and gets you started in the morning. Try adding some seasonal fruit, compote, or preserves.

8 CUPS (750 G) MUESLI
¾ cup (125 g) oats
¾ cup (125 g) rye
3 oz (80 g) pumpkin seeds
3 oz (80 g) sunflower seeds
3 oz (80 g) flax seeds
1 oz (25 g) sesame seeds
1 oz (25 g) shaven or shredded coconut
1¾ oz (50 g) pistachios
1¾ cup (50 g) whole almonds
1 oz (25 g) muscovado sugar
2½ tbsp (50 g) honey
½ cup (100 g/100 ml) warm water
2 tbsp (45 g/50 ml) cooking oil
3 oz (80 g) sun-dried fruit

1. Preheat the oven at 285°F (140°C).
2. Mix seeds, grains, and nuts in a bowl.
3. Pour the muscovado sugar on top of the mix.

4. In a cooking pot, combine the warm water with the honey and the cooking oil and heat the mixture while stirring constantly. Make sure it does not boil. It's only meant to stay warm (120–140°F/50–60°C).
5. Pour the honey mixture over the dry mix and blend gently with your hands.
6. Spread the muesli evenly on top of a baking sheet covered with parchment paper. Roast in the oven for 1½–2 hours. Stir with a wooden spoon every now and again to ensure that the mixture does not stick together. Remove the muesli from the oven and let it cool.
7. Add the dried fruit. I prefer currants, dried cherries, apricots, and pineapple, but any dried fruit will do well with this mixture.
8. Pour the muesli into a large metal container with tight sealing lid and store it in the kitchen cabinet.

In the small village of Selles-sur-Cher, known for its cheeses with the same name, Marie-Frédérique Peré and her husband Noël run a goat farm and a small cheese store. They manage everything as a team, from caring for the goats to crafting the cheese, which they sell at the village market.

With only one antler, the white Blanchette stands out from the other goats.

Some amazing cheeses from the farm. The round ones are Selles-sur-Cher cheeses, while the pyramid-shaped cheese is called Sainte-Maure. Making cheese is an art form—just like making sourdough bread—and the method to making cheese is protected by AOC-markings (Appellation d'Origine Contrôlée), which guarantees that all steps in the process are performed in the correct way. Imagine if this guarantee could be provided for sourdough bread!

THE BAKER'S FOOD

Chefs cannot bake bread and bakers cannot cook food. This is a fact that proves true 99 percent of the time. But at the same time, there are dishes that bakers actually have more success with than chefs. These are simple and earthy dishes that usually include bread as a base or that are prepared slowly and thoughtfully in an oven.

In this chapter, I will share with you some of my best recipes for complete happiness and joy while cooking and then savoring the finished dishes.

YOU ARE
WHAT YOU EAT

In third grade, I had a biology teacher who was truly a teacher's teacher. She had a very special way of explaining all sorts of processes that happen inside our bodies. Every class with her was like a show, and I always tried to get a front row seat to make sure I didn't miss anything. One of my most powerful memories of her was when she walked into the class room one day, dressed like a magician, and said, "I am a magician and I am going to transform a carrot into a rabbit." In her left hand was a carrot and in the right one, she held a cute, white rabbit by its ears. The class broke out in laughter, but our teacher remained completely serious. She put the rabbit on the desk and put the carrot next to it, which the rabbit started eating right away. "Taadaaa!" our teacher said. "You see, I have now transformed a carrot into a rabbit." What our teacher was showing us in that moment was something so elementary and obvious that most people forget it completely: A rabbit chewing a carrot produces saliva containing enzymes. The enzymes and the stomach acids in turn break down the food in our stomachs into smaller particles for absorption in our intestines. In our intestines, the nutrition comes in contact with our blood and, in the end, the blood provides the nutrition from the carrot to various parts of the body. Voilà the carrot has indeed become the ears, eyes, and paws of the rabbit; and if there was no carrot, there would be no rabbit. It works the same way for us humans; we are what we eat and we are all magicians transforming food into life. The story about the rabbit and the carrot is in many ways the foundation to my philosophy on food. It's important to me that there is a person and knowledge behind all the ingredients we eat, cook, and bake with. Unfortunately, as of late, the industry has done everything in its power to compete with this process. Sadly, the result is products that are filled with unnatural additives to prolong shelf life and enhance flavors.

INDUSTRIAL ADDITIVES

When speaking about additives and about industrially produced food and bread, it is important to remember that additives are rarely dangerous in themselves, but rather they are dangerous in what they hide. Good quality ingredients seldom need additives. There is no need to add artificial blueberry flavor if a natural, great blueberry taste is already there. There is no need to add ascorbic acid or extra gluten in flour of high quality. The additives only become necessary when the basic ingredients are of lower quality. The industry almost always tries to forgo the rules of nature to increase shelf life, taste, and, naturally, profits. But with each step taken, new problems are created, and these have to be solved with even more additives. To keep the bread from drying out after only a few days, fat can be added as a preventative measure. Voilà, now we have a new problem; the fat changes the flavor of the bread, and to compensate, sugar or molasses is added. New needs arise as soon as the previous one has been resolved, and a downward spiral of additives will conclude in the product we find on the supermarket shelves. The result? An end product with additives that hide rather than showcase what the product actually is. While the industrial supply chain is pedaling between logistics, cost, demand, and longevity, craftsmanship is about the complete opposite. A baker beginning with water, flour, and salt will create a product based on these simple ingredients. The ingredients lead the way from nature to the finished product.

INDUSTRIALISM, NATURE, AND GENETICALLY MODIFIED ORGANISMS

Nature has evolved over millions of years, but for the last twenty or so, people have tried to regulate the laws of nature in a frightful manner—by using genetically modified organisms. Advocates speak of GMO crops as a solution to world hunger and population growth; unfortunately, this is an equation that does not reflect reality. It's not the starving populations that benefit from GMO crops, but rather a few large commercial corporations.

By changing the natural growth cycle of a plant—and its DNA—the industry has developed plants that are resistant to specific pesticides. This makes it possible for farmers to spray their crops to eliminate weeds and insects without harming the crop. But to release GMO plants into nature is not only irreversible, it opens the possibility of changing our ecosystem permanently.

In many cases, these weeds have already developed their own resistance to the pesticides, and to handle this problem, many farmers are now forced to increase the dosage of these pesticides, which contain glyphosate, when they spray their crops. What was initially meant to be a solution has become a new problem in need of a new solution.

102

In addition to this, it is impossible to control the spreading of GMOs. Plant genes are spread through pollen, and we simply do not know what consequences the spread of GMOs may have in the future. We are risking an unwanted spread of GMOs that can threaten natural development and balance.

But nature is not the only one that pays a heavy price for our GMO crops. Behind the new crops are a few multinational corporations that have more or less monopolized the market by filing patents on the seeds that are part of our communal heritage. Many farmers are no longer allowed to use their own seeds and are now stuck in a vicious cycle in which they are forced to buy new seeds, along with their pesticide, from the large corporations every year.

Letting industrialism steer nature instead of letting nature develop our produce as it was meant to be is surely walking down the wrong path. When we start manipulating nature in an unnatural way, it's difficult to know what the long-term consequences might be for nature, for our health, and for evolution. Industrialized farming based on chemicals and genetically modified crops will cost us dearly, and as of yet, no one has any idea what that price will be.

THE FRENCH MEAL

Not so long ago, United Nations Educational, Scientific, and Cultural Organization (UNESCO) listed the French meal as a piece of cultural heritage that ought to be preserved. Perhaps it stems from the French meal being so much more than just food; the social aspect of the meal is just as important. To eat is to enjoy, and the dinner is an event that is meant to take time and last for hours.

The traditional French meal always begins with an aperitif and ends with a digestif. In between, four courses are served: appetizer, main course, cheese plate, and dessert.

Even if *l'aperitif* (also called *apéro*) is the start of the French meal, sometimes you'll only get an aperitif. I remember how surprised my wife at the time was on the first occasion we were offered an aperitif without dinner. In France, it's perfectly fine and actually quite common to serve only refreshments and snacks. You can drink practically anything as an aperitif; there are no particular rules except that you would never drink cognac or calvados as an aperitif. They belong to the digestif category and are always served after the meal. I prefer wines that are strong and sweet such as Banyuls, Pommeau, or Pineau, but I would not turn down a glass of cold champagne either.

With the aperitif, *amouse-bouche* are served, which translates to "to entertain the mouth." A perfect amouse-bouche should surprise and tease the taste buds. It can be either sweet or savory, and don't be surprised if you are served petit choux filled with duck liver paté, as well as vanilla macaroons. The snacks don't have to be complicated; the most important thing is for it to match the drink. My favorite amouse-bouche (and one that is easy to make) is a thin, lightly toasted baguette with some tapenade on top. It will certainly whet your appetite!

But what about on a regular day? The day is already hectic, so it's important for me to remove all stress surrounding the meal. If you have time to spend cooking, do so. But if you're tired and stressed, just put a nice piece of bread on the table with an assortment of cheeses, rouille, or pistou, some olives, and a nice glass of wine for dinner.

Here are some of my favorite meals from the French kitchen; some are more complicated and take time, while others are simple and fairly quick to prepare. The dishes do have one thing in common though; they all require ingredients of high quality.

BOUILLABAISSE

Bouillabaisse is more than a dish. It's a lifestyle that brings people together. This dish was originally made by fishermen and consisted of fish they could not sell at the market in Marseille. With time, bouillabaisse went from being a popular but simple dish to becoming one of luxury. Unfortunately, most of the fish from the original recipe are endangered today and are difficult to find on the market. On the next page, you will therefore find a modern version with fish and seafood that can easily be found in stores today.

12 LARGE PORTIONS

7 lbs (3 kg) mixed fish, i.e. John Dory, monkfish, scorpion fish, Great weever, Red gurnard, and mullet

1 orange

¾ cup (180 g/200 ml) olive oil

10 tomatoes, coarsely chopped

2 trimmed and coarsely chopped heads of fennel

5 onions, coarsely chopped

2 leeks, coarsely chopped

2 garlic cloves, peeled and finely chopped

2 red chilis, finely chopped

1 parsley plant, finely chopped

4 bay leaves

15 black peppercorns

coarse sea salt

16–20 cups (4–5 liters) water

3 tsp (1 g) saffron *or* 1½ oz (40 g) pickled saffron (pg. 157)

2 lbs (1 kg) peeled small, firm potatoes

1. Peel the orange with a potato peeler.

2. Heat the olive oil in a large cast-iron pot. At low heat, sauté tomatoes, fennel, onions, chilis, and orange peel, along with all the spices, except for the saffron, at low heat. Place the lid on the pot and let the mixture simmer for 15 minutes.

3. Clean, remove heads, and fillet all fish, except the Red gurnard and mullet.

4. Turn up the heat on the stove and add the fish to the pot. Simmer for a few minutes and then add the water. (Make sure that the water does not reach the top of the pot. If it does, the pot is too small for this recipe.) Close the lid and let simmer for another 20–30 minutes until the vegetables have softened.

5. Remove the pot from the heat and blend the mixture with a hand mixer. Strain the soup with a rotary strainer.

6. Add the saffron and let the bouillabaisse come to a boil. Reduce heat and let it simmer for another couple of minutes. Add the potatoes and let the soup simmer at low heat without the lid until the potatoes are almost soft.

7. Cut the fish fillets into even pieces and add them along with the Red gurnard and mullet just before serving. The fish should not be cooked in the broth and should only be poached slightly.

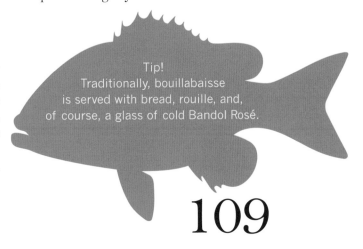

Tip!
Traditionally, bouillabaisse is served with bread, rouille, and, of course, a glass of cold Bandol Rosé.

109

CONTEMPORARY BOUILLABAISSE

Since most of the fish in the original recipe are endangered today,
I have created an alternative recipe here.

12 LARGE PORTIONS
1 batch bouillabaisse, pg. 109 (without the fish)
6 lbs (2½ kg) mixed fish, i.e. perch, walleye, and haddock
12 mussels with shells
shells from 1–2 lobsters
shells from 6 langoustines

Prepare as in the original recipe but exchange the fish for perch, walleye, and
haddock along with 12 mussels. Add the lobster and langoustine shells when
you add the fish. Take the opportunity to make a lovely salad from the lobster
and langoustine meat and serve it as an appetizer to the bouillabaisse.

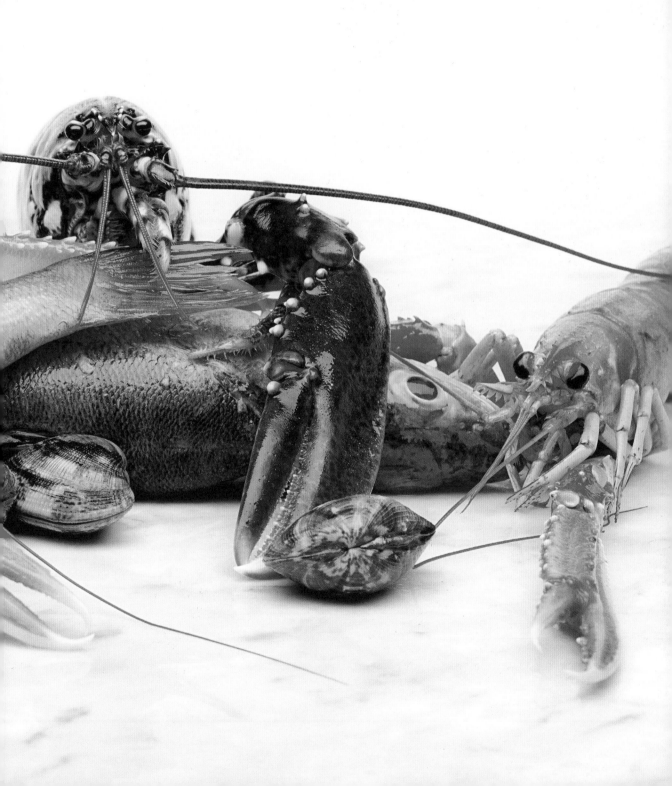

It's almost impossible not to be seduced by a really great Confit de Canard—a signature dish from the south of France that comes with an ancient heritage. In the small village of Castillon-d'Arthez, in the south of France, Juliette Prat-Bardiau has dedicated her life to breeding a limited number of the unusual species Lou Metche. Lou Metche ducks are more robust than other ducks and have unusual markings with blue-green wing tips.

CONFIT
DE CANARD

Confit is an ancient way of conserving and cooking, and it does miracles to the flavors. Meat gets tender and wonderfully fat in flavor. The confit consists of salting meat and then slowly simmering it in duck fat. It tastes great with a small portion of pommes salardaises or gratin dauphinois (potatoes au gratin). And with it, of course, the fantastic duck sauce . . .

6 PORTIONS

6 fatty duck thighs
1 handful coarse sea salt
1 pot thyme
1 pot rosemary
1 head of garlic, wedged and peeled
10 whole black peppercorns
5 bay leaves
2 cups (450 g) duck fat
a stable oven that can keep a consistent
    temperature of 195°F (90°C)

RED WINE DUCK SAUCE

1 bottle red wine (750 ml)
2 cups (500 g/500 ml) orange juice
all the juice from the confit
¼ cup (50 g) duck fat
fleur de sel (fine sea salt)
freshly ground black pepper

DAY 1

1. Rub the duck thighs with coarse sea salt, thyme, rosemary, and a couple of garlic cloves. Rub with vigor; the duck skin is thick and the salt and spices need to penetrate both the skin and meat thoroughly.
2. Place the duck thighs pressed together in an ovenproof dish (save the spices for later). Cover the dish with plastic wrap and let it rest in the fridge for 12 hours. This will prevent the meat from falling apart when you make the confit.

DAY 2

1. Scrape the salt off the duck thighs with the help of a rosemary stem. *Note:* Do not rinse the thighs with water—leave some salt on the thighs.
2. Preheat the oven to 195°F (90°C).
3. Place the duck thighs in the oven pan and layer in the spices. Spread the duck fat evenly over the meat.
4. Put the pan in the oven and let it simmer for 48 hours. The meat is supposed to "sweat" but not cook; if it cooks, turn down the heat slightly.

DAY 4

Hopefully the duck thighs now have a nice, brown color. Cover the pan with aluminum foil and turn off the oven. Let it cool down for 12 hours.

DAY 5

1. Place the duck thighs in a new oven pan. Separate the fat from the juices left at the bottom of the used pan. The juices will be the foundation for the sauce later on. You can store the fat in a sealed plastic container as it will last for several years and can be used any time, as many times as you wish, as long as it does not get boiled.
2. *Prepare the sauce:* Boil the wine and orange juice together with the duck juices from the confit. Let the sauce reduce to a fifth of its original volume. Add the duck fat and mix vigorously with a hand mixer. Season with salt and pepper.

115

LAMB ROAST

In this dish, the flavorful bone of the lamb takes center stage. The best and most flavorful lamb can be found on the island of Mont Saint-Michel, on the border of Brittany and Normandy. The lambs feed on salty fields consisting of grass and algae mix (the fields are covered by sea water half the time) and they are therefore naturally salty. Try to keep an interior meat temperature of 130°F (55°C) since there is really no need to kill an animal twice.

12 PORTIONS
1 leg of lamb at 7 lbs (3 kg)
1 head of garlic, wedged and peeled +
  2 cloves
1 stem thyme
1 stem rosemary
1 handful coarse sea salt
7 oz (200 g) of butter
10 bay leaves
freshly ground black pepper
3½ lbs (1 ½ kg) firm, large potatoes, peeled
1–1⅓ cups (200–300 ml) water

RED WINE SAUCE
2 large, finely chopped shallots
3½ oz (100 g) butter
3 bay leaves
10 black peppercorns
1 bottle of red wine (750 ml)

1. Preheat the oven to 330°F (165°C). Make small, deep pockets in the meat with the help of a fillet knife and insert the garlic cloves. Rub the meat thoroughly with sea salt, thyme, and rosemary.
2. Heat up a large pot with half the butter and place the meat in the pot along with all the spices (even the ones you rubbed the meat with). Sear the meat at high heat all around for a few minutes. Place the meat in an ovenproof pan.

3. Add the rest of the butter to the pot and fry the potatoes at high heat for a few minutes with two crushed cloves of garlic, salt, pepper, and parsley.
4. Place the potatoes around the roast. Pour the water all over and bake in the oven until the meat has an interior temperature of 130°F (55°C). Stir the potatoes every so often to make sure they don't burn. Add more water if the pan gets too dry.
5. *Prepare the sauce:* Sautee the shallots at low heat with half the butter. Add bay leaves and peppercorns. When the shallots are soft and transparent, pour the wine into the pot. Let simmer until the sauce has reduced to a fifth in volume. Sift the sauce and add the remaining butter just before serving. Mix with a hand blender.

Tip!
I often cook meat in the oven and treat it just as I would sourdough bread. It's always good to add moisture to the oven. Place a pot of water on the bottom of the oven and refill with water during the cooking process. That way, the meat will be juicier.

A Frenchman in Sweden.

A Swedish Frenchman

I remember when I called one of my closest relatives only a few days after I had moved to Sweden. My cousin laughed heartily at me and in only a few minutes, he had uttered quite a few clichés about Sweden and the Swedes: I really should consider carrying a weapon because you never know if I would run into a polar bear when walking down the city streets. I would never need to order ice with my whiskey since the whole bar would surely be encased in it anyway! I got irritated and the conversation ended quickly.

People who only see as far in front of them as their noses truly annoy me. It only gets worse when these people judge matters they have no experience with and certainly don't understand. I love my home country and the French culture, but in Sweden I was able to find something I have never found anywhere else (and in great abundance): openness, a life with balanced nature, and a respect for society. I am filled with pride when I tell other people that I live in Sweden, and I feel privileged to have found my way here.

But in the beginning, it was pretty difficult to get used to all the new things. Something as simple as shopping for milk demanded so much effort, and proud as I am, I refused to ask for help. It took several trips to the supermarket and many pints of sour milk, yogurt, and oat milk before I got it right and could prepare a real café au lait.

Finding a job was not that easy either. I was used to getting a job within days of starting my search. In Stockholm, it took a lot longer. I walked the city from bakery to bakery and from restaurant to restaurant. At the bakeries I was told that I was not competent enough since I had never made cinnamon rolls or hadn't even heard of Princess Cake. At the restaurants I got the same refrain, "Unfortunately, we do not have a pastry chef position here . . . The cold buffet staff create our desserts and we buy bread from a bakery that delivers."

After a few weeks of looking without any success, I walked down to the unemployment office at Södermalm. There was a dusty binder with a few employment ads for people who didn't speak Swedish. I finally found the telephone number for David Negri, head chef at the Strand Hotel by Nybrokajen, and he hired me right away. Unfortunately, not as a pastry chef or baker but as a fish cook in the restaurant. After scaling, de-boning, and filleting a whole bunch of salmon that first day, I could still smell salmon scales on my skin, even after several showers.

The job as a fish cook only lasted for a few days; at that time David realized that my place really was in the bakery. It was time to end the era of the industrially made bread served to guests during the breakfast buffet.

All cooks in the kitchen spoke English with one another just that so I could understand and be a part of the camaraderie. Fascinating! Imagine a crew of French chefs in a French restaurant speaking English just to accommodate a foreign baker.

At the same time, it did hinder my attempts at learning Swedish, and the language and culture do go together. If you can't speak the language, you can't really understand the culture. After two years of communicating in English, I finally decided to learn Swedish. Today, I think of all the people forced to listen to my Swedish—I barely knew fifty words!

Now, I feel like I have embraced Swedish culture and in some magical way managed to fuse it with my own French culture. I got the best of two worlds—an unbeatable combination. I have become a Frenchman in Stockholm!

123

MONSIEUR & MADAME CROQUE

On one of my first food experiences in Sweden, I ordered a Croque Monsieur, but to my great surprise, there was a slice of pineapple under the cheese! I went over to the cashier and asked why there was pineapple on a Croque Monsieur. The waitress apologized and said: "Oh, we have made a mistake. You got a Croque Madame instead . . ." The smooth and creamy béchamel sauce restores the moisture within the bread to its original state. Fast, easy, and so incredibly delicious.

6 MONSIEUR CROQUE

12 thin sourdough slices
6 thick ham slices
3 cups (300 g) shredded cheese, preferably
    gruyère or comté

BÉCHAMEL SAUCE

2 cups (500 g/500 ml) milk
a pinch of salt
freshly ground black pepper
2 oz (50 g) unsalted butter
a knife's edge of fresh nutmeg
⅓ cup (50 g) flour
1½ cups (150 g) shredded comté or
    emmenthal cheese

1. Preheat the oven to 450°F (240°C).
2. *Prepare the béchamel sauce:* Heat up the milk with a pinch of salt and black pepper in a pot at low heat. Be careful not to burn it.
3. In another pot, melt the butter and add a little bit of fresh nutmeg while stirring constantly. Sift the flour into the melted butter.
4. Add the milk, a little at a time, into the flour and butter mix and stir more vigorously.
5. When all the milk has been added, remove the pot from the burner. If the sauce is too thick, just add a little bit more milk (flour reacts in many different ways and some absorb more liquid than others).
6. Stir in the shredded cheese and season with salt and pepper.
7. Place six pieces of bread on a baking sheet covered with parchment paper. Spread a dollop of béchamel sauce on each piece. Place a slice of ham on top and sprinkle some shredded cheese over it. Finish by placing another piece of bread on top. Add a dollop of béchamel sauce and top it off with some shredded cheese.
8. Bake your Croque in the oven until the cheese has melted and gotten a nice color. Serve with green salad and Dijon mustard.

MADAME CROQUE
In my Croque Madame, you will not find any pineapple! Follow the above recipe but add a freshly fried egg after baking.

125

1. Heat the milk with salt and pepper. In another pot, melt the butter with some fresh nutmeg.

2. Sift the flour into the melted butter while whisking.

3. Add the warm milk, a little bit at a time, into the flour and butter mix and whisk vigorously.

4. Remove the pot from the burner and add the shredded cheese while stirring. Season with salt and pepper.

PISSALADIÈRE

Pissaladière is not just any ordinary pizza. It's a pizza from Nice—where they have the best street food in the world. The ingredients are wonderfully simple, the onion is made into confit with either duck fat or olive oil, and the pizza is topped off with arugula and tasty vinaigrette. It doesn't matter if the baguette dough is leavened for too long—the results turn out even better if it is!

6 PORTIONS
2½–3 cups (500–600 g) baguette dough
  (pg. 78)
6 large yellow onions
3 oz (100 g) duck fat *or* olive oil
4–5 bay leaves
freshly chopped thyme
freshly chopped rosemary
⅓–¾ cup (100–200 ml) Nice olives
1 can sardines in olive oil (2 oz/55 g)
arugula
a splash of vinaigrette (pg. 149)

1. Turn the oven to the highest heat, preferably with a baking stone. middle rack
2. Peel and slice the onions.
3. Melt the duck fat in a frying pan on low heat. Confit the onions with the spices. Confit is created when the liquid from the onions slowly evaporates and is replaced by the lovely duck fat. Remove the pot from the heat when the onions are transparent and soft, making sure that they are not brown or crispy.
4. Roll the baguette dough very thin and put it on a greased baking sheet or directly onto a baking peel. Spread out the confit onions. (Remove the bay leaves and spices if you like—I prefer to leave them in.)
5. Spread the olives and sardines on top.
6. Rub the dough edges with some oil from the can of sardines and bake in the middle of the oven at the highest possible heat until the edges get a nice color.
7. Cut *la pissaladière* into large pieces, adding plenty of arugula salad, and spread a little bit of vinaigrette on top. Fold and enjoy!

Dough that has leavened too much is a result of either leavening too fast or for too long. The end result is dough that sinks because the gluten web has collapsed.

129

LE GRATIN Á LA SALARDAISE

I love the term "au gratin"—so French and so Swedish at the same time. The potato is the root vegetable recipes use most in Swedish cookbooks, and here is one more for your collection. Porcini mushrooms can be substituted for chanterelles or, when they are out of season, regular mushrooms will do just fine.

6 PORTIONS
3 lbs (1½ kg) firm potatoes
2 tbsp (50 g) duck fat
2 garlic cloves
4 cups (200 g) porcini mushrooms
1 handful finely chopped parsley
4 cups (1000 g/1 liter) heavy cream
sea salt
freshly ground black pepper

1. Preheat the oven to 350°F (180°C).
2. Peel and slice the potatoes thinly. Leave the slices in the sink under the running water for a few minutes to allow the starch to wash away.
3. Heat the duck fat in a frying pan. Crush the garlic and fry it in the duck fat with the porcini mushrooms. Add the parsley at the end. Set the pan aside for the time being.
4. Grease an ovenproof dish with some duck fat. Layer the potatoes and porcini mushrooms in rows until the whole dish is covered.
5. Pour the heavy cream, salt, and pepper into the frying pan. Let it reach a boil and then simmer for a few minutes. The flavors will become concentrated and the cream will absorb the flavor of the mushrooms.
6. Pour the cream on top the potatoes. Cover the dish with aluminum foil and bake in the middle of the oven for 1 hour. Reduce the temperature to 325°F (160°C), remove the foil, and let it bake for another 30 minutes.

FRENCH PANCAKES

French pancakes are a little sweeter, greasier, and thinner than other pancakes. Vanilla, rum, or orange blossom water is a must, however. The sourdough is just a plus to give extra flavor. Preferably, the batter should be allowed to rest overnight, but sometimes this isn't possible. If you're in a hurry, it's enough to let the batter rest for an hour or so. At my house, we always begin our pancake dinner with a meatier variation, which includes cheese, ham, and a dollop of crème fraîche. It's a good idea to divide the batter before you add the rum or orange blossom water, as those sweet tastes do not work well with meatier pancakes.

20 PANCAKES
3 cups (400 g) wheat flour
2 pinches of salt
3 oz (50 g) sugar
a small dollop of sourdough to taste
1½ oz (50 g) light beer
seeds from one vanilla bean *or* 1½ oz rum
    or a few drops orange blossom water
4 (7 oz/200 g) eggs
1½ cups (400 g/400 ml) milk
½ cup (150 g/150 ml) water
3 oz (100 g) melted butter + butter for
    frying

DAY 1
1. Mix flour, salt, and sugar in a bowl. Add sourdough, beer, and possibly seeds from a vanilla bean. (If you choose to flavor with rum or orange blossom water, wait until day 2.)
2. Add the eggs and then the milk, a little bit at a time. Whisk until the batter is smooth.

3. Add the water and stir, then add the melted butter. Whisk vigorously.
4. Cover the bowl with a baking towel and let the batter rest in the fridge overnight.

DAY 2
1. By now, the batter should have thickened a bit. Check the consistency to make sure it's still thin enough. If the batter is too thick, simply add a little bit of milk.
2. If you are making a sweeter version, you can now add rum or orange blossom water while stirring. If not, just omit this step.
3. Activate your pancake-making autopilot and begin frying your crêpes with a little butter on each side.
4. Serve either as a meaty dish with cheese, ham, and crème fraîche, or as a sweet finish to your dinner.

132

CRÊPES SUZETTE

If you prefer a more luxurious version, try making crêpes Suzette. Fry the crêpe on both sides. Remove from the heat and spread a thin layer of crème pâtissière (pg. 234) on top. Fold the crêpe in half and flambé in Grand Marinier when serving. Top it off with some orange zest. Et voilà!

QUICHE LORRAINE

duck fat

Pie filled with egg royal, smoked bacon, and onions. The recipe originates in the northeast of France, in Lorraine, but there are thousands of variations depending on season, mood, and of course, what you have in the fridge. If you happen to have a jar of duck fat at home, you can thank your lucky stars. Use the fat in the filling instead of butter—it will taste amazing. Serve with a green salad for a delectable lunch!

2 QUICHE PIE CRUSTS
4 cups (500 g) wheat flour
9 oz (250 g) unsalted butter
a pinch of sea salt
2–3 oz (3½ oz/125 g) eggs
3½ oz (50 g/50 ml) water

EGG ROYAL
6 (11 oz/300 g) eggs
3 cups (700 g/700 ml) heavy cream
sea salt
freshly ground black pepper

FILLING
3 oz (75 g) butter *or* canola oil
    (or better yet, duck fat)
1 tsp raw sugar
3 onions, finely chopped
10 oz (300 g) smoked bacon, cubed

DAY 1
Mix flour, butter, and salt in a large bowl until you have dough with a grainy consistency. Add eggs and water. Knead the dough until it is nice and smooth. Wrap the dough in plastic wrap and let it rest overnight in the fridge.

DAY 2
1. Crack the eggs for the egg mixture in a bowl and add the heavy cream while whisking. Season with salt and pepper to taste. Place the bowl in the fridge.
2. Heat the fat for the filling in a frying pan and add the raw sugar. Stir until the sugar caramelizes. Fry the onions in the fat until they become a golden brown color. Remove the onions and quickly fry the bacon in the same pan.
3. Preheat the oven to 400°F (200°C).
4. Roll the dough thinly and drape it inside the two greased dishes, about 10 inches (26 cm) in diameter. Spread the onions and the bacon atop the dough. Slowly pour the egg royal on top, but leave about half an inch of the edge free.
5. Bake in the middle of the oven for 30–45 minutes or until the egg royal has solidified.

VEGGIES!
Replace the bacon with butter sautéed beetroots, mushrooms, or other vegetables generously seasoned with salt, black pepper, and fresh herbs.

135

CASSOULET

This is a legendary dish, and it's also a hot topic all over France. Every small village has its own recipe and both Castelnaudary and Toulouse claim to have created the original. During the extended baking time, the crust has to be broken every thirty minutes. It is called casser la croute, which is also slang for "to eat." In a real cassoulet, time and attention are the two most important ingredients.

10 LARGE PORTIONS
2¼ lbs (1 kg) cocoa beans *or* mogette beans
1 small ham hock, bone in
1 yellow onion with 5 cloves inserted
2½ cups (500 g) duck or goose fat
2 garlic cloves
7 oz (200 g) smoked bacon, cubed
2 large carrots, peeled and sliced diagonally
2 bouquet garni (pg. 154)
1 French garlic sausage
6 Toulouse sausages
1 chopped yellow onion
5 tomatoes sliced in halves
1 fresh espelette pepper *or* 1 red chili pepper
6 confit duck thighs, deboned (pg. 115, up
   to day 4)
sea salt
plenty of freshly ground black pepper

DAY 1
Soak both the beans and the ham hock (separately) in plenty of cold water overnight.

DAY 2
1. Let the ham hock drain completely on paper towels.
2. Divide the onion in halves and fry the pieces in a large pot with a heaping spoonful of duck or goose fat for a few minutes. Add a crushed garlic clove, smoked bacon, and carrots. Add the beans and 1 bouquet garni and cover with lightly salted water. Let simmer over low heat for 1 hour.
3. Cut the garlic sausage into half-inch (1 cm) slices. Fry them in a large pot along with the Toulouse sausage, one garlic clove, one bouquet garni, the chopped onion, tomatoes, and a large spoonful of duck or goose fat. When it starts to color, pour a few spoonfuls of broth from the bean casserole and let it simmer for one more hour.

Tip!
As with most stews, Cassoulet always tastes better the day after it's cooked.

136

4. Boil the ham hock in a pot with fresh water until the meat falls off the bone. This should take about 1 hour. Rinse the meat and shred it into small pieces. Add the ham hock to the stew.

5. Preheat the oven to 330°F (165°C).

6. Cut the duck thighs into smaller pieces in a *cassoule* (a large pan that looks like a casserole pan). Create a layer of sausage and ham hock stew and then cover with a layer of duck confit. Repeat until the cassoule is filled (save the stock from the beans). Top it off with the rest of the duck or goose fat.

7. Place the cassoule in the oven and carefully stir it once every thirty minutes to break the crust on top. Pour some bean stock into it once in a while to ensure that the cassoule does not get dry. If you run out of stock, you can use water instead (never use any other liquid). After 3–4 hours, the cassoule is ready.

SMART
SEASONAL FOOD

In olden times, people had to eat with the seasons. But now most produce is available throughout the year, and it's easy to deviate from this cycle. However, eating off-season produce costs more money and the flavors are often not as good. Food tastes better and is cheaper if you respect the produce seasons; you'll pay less for good quality items. Off-season products also have a greater impact on the environment since they often need to be transported farther and must be artificially heated to grow. Since we can buy almost anything at any time now—especially within the bigger cities—our knowledge of seasonal produce is decreasing. My favorite time is August, when the apricots, pears, and figs taste the best. Since many of us don't know enough about what products are the best and at what time of the year—both when it comes to Swedish and foreign produce—I have compiled a simple guide for you to follow to make smarter decisions about seasonal food.

WINTER PRODUCE
December–March
It's most difficult to eat nutritious seasonal food during the winter. Take advantage of root vegetables, such as artichokes, turnips, carrots, and parsnips, as well as Brussels sprouts and green cabbage, since these products can be stored for longer periods of time than, say, tomatoes or iceberg lettuce. Also, take advantage of the citrus fruits imported from the Mediterranean. Swedish winter apples are another alternative in January. March is a challenging month when it comes to fruits and vegetables. The primary produce has not arrived yet and the winter citrus fruit season is at an end. Hold on!

PRIMARY PRODUCE OF SPRING
April–June
Spring is the height of the primary produce season, but sometimes we're too eagerly longing for asparagus, fresh potatoes, and other openly grown vegetables. These items are still expensive rarities in April, so it's better to spend your money on lettuce and nettles. We can finally enjoy asparagus, rhubarb, and fresh potatoes in May and June. This is also the high season for onions all over Europe.

SUMMER FLAVORS
July–September
This is the time for plenty of fresh, locally produced food. Enjoy artichokes, cucumbers, zucchini, tomatoes, and fruits and berries such as raspberries, blueberries, melons, nectarines, and peaches.

FALL: HARVEST TIME
October–November
This is when it's cheapest to enjoy root vegetables, mushrooms, and potatoes. The Swedish plum season is short. And in contrast to what most people think, figs are at their best during fall—not at Christmas, when most of them are imported from Brazil.

139

Early Saturday morning at the already-buzzing vegetable market in Pau. The sellers are private individuals who rent the space to sell the fruits and vegetables freshly harvested from their private gardens and allotments.

Prix ▶ 2,50 €
1Kg
Prix ▶ 2,50
€
Produit : PATISSON
Variété : BIO
Origine : ASSAT
Calibre :
Catégorie

Even though Bernard has been retired for twenty years, he still continues to visit the store daily. His son, Jean-Luc, took over the store when Bernard retired. Bernard and Jean-Luc are involved in all steps of the business, from raising cattle to the final product on the shelves. Here he is, proudly holding up one of their Bayonne hams, which they air-dry for twelve months.

OILS & MIXTURES

I love old bottles and jars! It's so great to be able to give them a new life preserving fresh spices, a cup or two of cold-pressed olive oil, and a pinch of sea salt.

Mixtures make for perfect accompaniments to sourdough bread and are the easiest ways to enhance dishes. In this chapter, you'll also find some unbeatable tips on how to make your own preserves.

AROMATIC OILS

Dash a small amount of thyme oil on top of an avocado and forget winter completely. Aromatic oils are the best ways to preserve the flavors of summer for those cold winter nights. By pasteurizing the oils in the oven, the flavors of the spices will be even more enhanced and the shelf life will be extended.

To create your own aromatic oils, you don't need any recipes. All you need is a good variety of high-quality spices and then you can just get creative and start mixing. Some of my favorite flavors are espelette peppers, thyme, rosemary, tarragon, garlic, pink peppercorns, and ginger.

Do the following: Mix a handful of your favorite spices with olive oil and a pinch of sea salt (the salt enhances the flavors and extends the shelf life) in a glass bottle and seal it with a cork. Pasteurize the aromatic oils in the oven at 175–195°F (80–90°C) for a couple of hours. The oils are not meant to boil, only to be pasteurized, and this way, there will be no need to keep them in the fridge. Oils are always best kept at room temperature.

Tip! Create two indents in the cork so you can pour the oil without having to uncork it.

LA VINAIGRETTE

I don't like when oil and vinegar are sprinkled directly onto the salad. The proportions are never right and the flavors don't mix properly. At my house, I always make the vinaigrette first, directly in the salad bowl, so I can just fill it up with salad and mix it right before serving. It creates an incredible difference in flavor.

DRESSING 1 LARGE SALAD
1 shallot
1 tsp Dijon mustard
4 tbsp (50 ml) red wine vinegar
freshly ground black pepper
fleur de sel (fine sea salt)
½ cup (100 ml) cold pressed olive oil

Peel and finely chop the shallot. Mix all ingredients except for the oil. Add the oil a little at a time while whisking vigorously.

P.S. For fifteen years I have been making my own red wine vinegar at home. It is extremely easy and tastes so much better than the store-bought kind. To make your own red wine vinegar, you need a so-called mother. A "vinegar mother" is a culture of vinegar acid bacteria, which resembles calf liver. It takes a long time to produce, but if you are lucky, you might get some from a friend or on the Internet. Keep the vinegar mother in a vinegar pot of clay with a lid on and drain. Feed her consistently with good-quality wine leftovers.

LEMONETTE
Exchange the vinegar for
freshly squeezed lemon juice
and you will have a lemonette instead.

1 shallot
1 tsp Dijon mustard
4 tbsp (50 ml) freshly squeezed
lemon juice
½ cup (100 ml) cold-pressed olive oil
3–4 rotations of the black pepper mill
2 large pinches of fleur de sel
(fine sea salt)

Peel and finely chop the shallot.
Mix onion, Dijon, and lemon
juice in a bowl. Add olive oil, a
little at a time while whisking.
Season with salt
and pepper.

TAPENADE & PISTOU

Tapenade and pistou are two great mixtures perfectly suited for a piece of sourdough bread. The secret behind a great tapenade is to use high-quality olives. Olives from Nice are the best; they're difficult to core, but well worth the hassle. Serve the tapenade on a thin slice of toasted sourdough bread.

Pistou is a simple mixture that works with almost anything. Try spreading pistou on bread dough before you bake it, season chicken before you roast it, or bake fish dipped in pistou before adding the breadcrumbs. These mixtures last in the fridge for 2–3 months after the jar has been opened.

TAPENADE
4 cups (400 g) Nice olives
1 head of garlic
10 anchovies
20 small capers
1 cup (200–300 ml) cold-pressed olive oil

Core all olives. Wedge and peel the garlic. Mix all ingredients with a hand mixer. How much to mix is a matter of taste; some people like thick tapenade while others prefer it creamier. Store in a properly sealed clean glass jar and keep refrigerated.

PISTOU
1 pot of basil (approx. 3½ oz [100 g])
2 garlic cloves
1 pinch fleur de sel (fine sea salt)
freshly ground black pepper
1 cup (200 ml) cold-pressed olive oil

On a large wooden cutting board, finely chop the basil and garlic. When the herbs start to darken, add salt and pepper. Continue chopping until you have a creamy consistency. Pour the basil mixture into a glass jar. Add the olive oil and stir. Store in a clean glass jar and refrigerate.

151

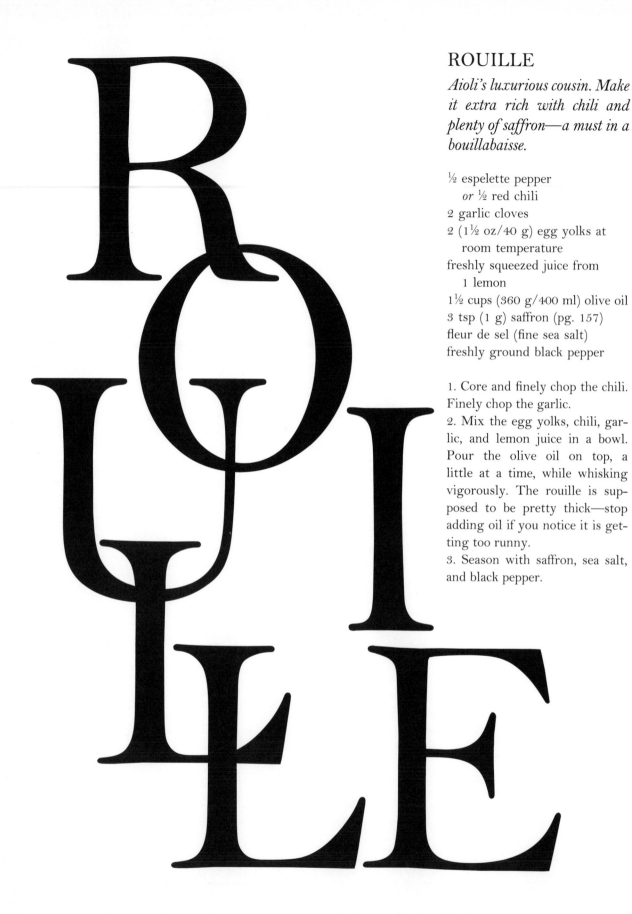

ROUILLE

Aioli's luxurious cousin. Make it extra rich with chili and plenty of saffron—a must in a bouillabaisse.

½ espelette pepper
   or ½ red chili
2 garlic cloves
2 (1½ oz/40 g) egg yolks at
   room temperature
freshly squeezed juice from
   1 lemon
1½ cups (360 g/400 ml) olive oil
3 tsp (1 g) saffron (pg. 157)
fleur de sel (fine sea salt)
freshly ground black pepper

1. Core and finely chop the chili. Finely chop the garlic.
2. Mix the egg yolks, chili, garlic, and lemon juice in a bowl. Pour the olive oil on top, a little at a time, while whisking vigorously. The rouille is supposed to be pretty thick—stop adding oil if you notice it is getting too runny.
3. Season with saffron, sea salt, and black pepper.

There are many varieties of rouille. Instead of emulsifying the egg yolk and oil, you can use bread drenched in milk overnight. I prefer the variety without milk.

BOUQUET GARNI

The words "bouquet garni" have many different meanings in French: a nice bouquet of flowers, the taste of wine, and the fragrance panel of the grand finale at the fireworks display—when the fireworks explode and light up the sky. In the world of gastronomy, the bouquet garni is a mix of herbs, spices, and vegetables tied together. Its multitude of fragrances and flavors get transferred into the food. Since they're tied together, it's so easy to pick them up when the dish is ready to serve. There is no original recipe for a bouquet garni. This is my version, which is perfectly suited for French dishes.

1 BOUQUET GARNI
1 stem bay leaves
1 stem rosemary
1 stem thyme
1 stem sage
1 stem parsley
the green part of a leek
1 stem celery leaves
a couple of bruised garlic cloves
½ onion with 3–4 cloves inserted in it
3 ft cooking string

Tie all ingredients together with the string.
Immerse the bouquet into your ragu, soup, or stew while cooking and remove it before serving.

PICKLED SAFFRON

Marinated saffron is an amazing seasoning for food, bread, condiments, and cookies. I prefer saffron when it is whole, as it's much easier to judge its quality when you can see the entire pistil. The problem with whole saffron pistils is that they are pretty dry and therefore don't flavor dough very well. I usually buy saffron from Iran or Afghanistan in January, when it's the cheapest and the best. I then immerse it in cognac and raw sugar, which serve as both flavor enhancers and preservatives, until its time for me to bake with it during the Christmas holidays. You can replace regular saffron with pickled saffron by exchanging 1 tsp ($^1/_2$ g) regular saffron for 3 tsp (10 g) pickled saffron.

7 OZ (200 grams) PICKLED SAFFRON
$^1/_3$ oz (10 g) saffron pistils
½ cup (100 g/100 ml) cognac
½ cup (100 g) raw sugar

Mix all ingredients and pour into a clean glass jar with a tight sealing lid. Refrigerate. The saffron can be used after only a couple of weeks, but it's best to let it marinate for several months to let the flavors develop completely.

Tip!
I usually buy saffron from Iran or Afghanistan.
When you buy saffron from Afghanistan, you also contribute to a good cause. The farmers there have begun to grow saffron as an alternative to opium. By selling saffron, they can free themselves from the drug trade and earn more money at the same time.

While driving from Paris to Pau—taking pictures for this cookbook—we encountered an amazing garden. We stopped and knocked on this man's door and asked if we could tour it. He turned out to be a renowned chef from Paris who had returned to Libourne to care for his elderly mother. Since his return, the garden has become his life's work. Here he grows sixteen different types of tomato, and the garden overflows with pear trees and the sweetest strawberries I have ever tasted.

CONFITURES

My mother is known as the queen of preserves. She has forty-five years of experience, and I am sure she has made preserves from practically everything edible. Everything from quince and green tomatoes to zucchini and rose petals. It was such a joy when she, in the middle of winter, came up from the cellar with a jar of *confiture de mûre* (blackberry preserves) or *gelée de groiselles à maquereaux* (gooseberry preserves). It always added sunshine to our breakfast and livened up any boring piece of bread.

There are many ways to make preserves. Since I bake plenty of bread at home, my kitchen oven is pimped out with a thick baking stone and the oven often has heat left over whenever I bake. Leftover heat is one of my favorite things. You can use it to roast nuts, dry bread, confit meat, make candied fruits, dry vanilla beans, and pasteurize juice.

Another wonderful way to use leftover heat is to make preserves in it. I use a large copper pot and let the leftover heat do the rest.

There is a difference between making preserves with fresh fruit versus frozen fruit. Fruits contain different levels of water, sugar, and, most importantly, pectin. This makes it difficult to have exact recipes for preserves. It is easier to succeed when cooking in the oven; the extended cooking period extracts the pectin from the fruit and the gentle heat prevents the preserves from burning. Another tip is to boil the fruit with the pits left inside them. It makes a big difference in flavor and consistency. Use a food mill to remove the pits in the end, before you fill the glass jars with preserves.

At my house, we eat a lot of preserves and we really have to fill those jars diligently to have enough for those dark winter months. The best preserves are made from fresh seasonal fruit, but of course it can be done with dried or frozen fruit as well (as long as you adjust the cooking method and the amount of sugar depending on the berries and fruits you use).

PRESERVES MADE FROM DRIED FRUITS AND BERRIES

Soak the fruit (for example figs, raisins, apricots, or plums) in warm water and let them rehydrate at room temperature for 12 hours. Drain the water that has not been absorbed by the fruit. Weigh the fruit and then add 30–40 percent of its weight in sugar.

Cover the pot with a baking towel and let it rest for another 12 hours. During the resting period, osmosis will set in (pg. 18) and will prepare the fruit for the last stage in the oven.

Cut out a piece of parchment paper that will fit the pot exactly and place it on top of the fruit so it is in direct contact with the fruit. Place the pot in the oven at 210°F (100°C) for 1 hour per pound (500 g) of preserves. It's fine if the oven is hotter than this in the beginning, as you may just have finished baking pastries or a few loaves of bread. Just be sure to stir the pot once in a while to ensure that the sugar does not stick to the bottom of the pot.

PRESERVES FROM FROZEN FRUITS AND BERRIES

If you choose to make strawberry preserves in January, it's much easier and of course much cheaper to buy frozen strawberries, which were picked at the height of their flavor and ripeness and were then frozen. There is nothing worse than thawed, mushy strawberries on top of a dessert, but they are great to make preserves with and work just as well as other fruits and berries.

The process is pretty much the same as for dried fruits except that the fruits or berries are not rehydrated. Weigh the fruit and then add 50 percent of the fruits' weight in sugar.

Let the fruit sit in the pot at room temperature for 24 hours, covered by a baking towel. Then, cut out a piece of parchment paper to place directly on top of the fruit. Place the pot in the oven at 210°F (100°C) for an hour and a half per pound of preserves. Stir once in a while to ensure that the sugar does not stick to the bottom of the pot.

PRESERVES FROM FRESH FRUITS AND BERRIES

I visit my favorite food market in central Stockholm just when all the small fruit and vegetable vendors are closing up for the night. This is when I find the best deals and I buy crates of ripe, and perhaps some bruised, fruits for next to nothing—perfect for making preserves.

Preserves made from fresh fruit are less sweet. By no means am I taking any stands against sugar (I'm a four sugar cubes in my coffee kind of guy), but when we use less sugar, the flavors from the fruit become so much more enhanced. I like when the consistency and sweetness resemble a compote, but has a clear preserves feeling.

Making preserves with fresh fruit is the same as before, but you reduce the sugar content to 30 percent of the fruit's weight to get the right consistency.

Cut a piece of parchment paper to fit snuggly on top of the fruit in the pot. Place the pot in the oven at 210°F (100°C) for an hour and a half per pound of preserves. Stir occasionally to make sure the sugar does not stick to the bottom of the pot.

Mom's Tip!
If your copper pan has a greenish layer before you use it, make sure to clean it out first. Brush the pot with sea salt and vinegar and it will be as good as new again.

There's no lack of guesthouses and inns in the French countryside. Here you can stay overnight or for weeks, and you can enjoy a genuine French meal—often with regional heritage. In Noyers-sur-Cher, you can find this family-managed guesthouse, called Hostellerie le Clos du Cher. From here, you can easily get to the nearby village Selles-sur-Cher, which is known for its cheeses.

L'école de pâtisserie

Pastry School

It was 1991, and I had just turned sixteen when I got the letter saying I had been accepted into the pastry school at Beauvais. The night before my first day, I had been working at my parents' bakery and, as the sun rose, I drove sleepily but full of excitement the six miles (ten km) on my red scooter to my first day of classes. I was the youngest one in my class and compared to all the other students, I was ecstatic at having been accepted. Besides myself, there were twenty-two boys between the ages of eighteen and twenty-two. Not one single girl was there, and not one other student seemed to be interested in the education or the profession at all. Later on, I came to realize what an ungrateful job it was to work as a pastry chef in France during the '90s. It was basically work that was handed out to people who couldn't do anything else. The two-year education was called *apprentissage*—apprenticeship—and to be accepted, you first had to find a maitre. A *maitre* was a pastry chef who was willing to hire you and make you his responsibility. He or she needed a certain license to take on an apprentice and also had to be approved by the school. It was then the maitre's responsibility to make sure that, after two years of apprenticeship, the student passed the final exam. If you failed, you had to redo a whole year and then take the exam again. If you failed a second time, you were expelled from school and the maitre would lose his or her license to teach any more students. My brother was my maitre and my father supervised us. My dad and my brother were complete opposites, and they always argued about everything, from how an éclair should taste to how a baguette should be baked, or if we should be open on Tuesdays or not. I think this shaped me into who I am today—never afraid of conflict and always ready to discuss whatever the issue might be. But perhaps the most important thing was that I learned the baking process from the ground up. To understand is the key to being in control. One person who helped me find that key was my pastry teacher Monsieur Leroux. Monsieur Leroux was my idol during my school years. He was a large, hairy red-headed Frenchman who could have been related to a grizzly bear. He was tough with all of us but always fair. What I loved the most about him was that he would always have answers to my questions. And he was the one who taught me that the things that seemed most simple were usually the most difficult. The first day we were supposed to cook *crème pâtissière* (vanilla cream), make apple pie, *brioche de Nanterre*, and cake base for *génoise*. That day

was the happiest day of my life. Since the day I started walking, the way a perfect crème pâtissière is meant to feel in your mouth had been instilled in me, along with the knowledge of how important it is to not get fancy when it comes to making apple pie. We started at eight o'clock in the morning and we were still there past nine at night, cleaning the whole bakery. The parents, who were getting worried at this point, had gathered outside the school, but Monsieur Leroux refused to let us go before we were done: "You always know when your day begins but not necessarily when it ends!" The students who failed to make the vanilla cream, the apple pie, brioche, or the cake base were not allowed to move forward to more complicated assignments and had to repeat these until they succeeded. Monsieur Leroux's words again: "You cannot make a sugar sculpture if you cannot first make a perfect apple pie." After the first year, Monsieur Leroux and the school principal allowed me to take the test that would make me an officially certified pastry chef. I got the highest score in the whole school. Not because my sugar sculpture was the nicest but because it had soul. Not because my apple pie was the best looking but because it tasted great. To this day, this is the one of the most important aspects of baking I have learned.

168

169

SWEET BREAD

Croissants, pain au chocolat, and chausson aux pommes—these breads are called viennoiseries in France. They are delicate, sweet, and crispy pastries great for dipping in coffee, tea, or hot chocolate for breakfast. With milk, sugar, egg, wheat flour, and butter as a foundation, they are pretty easy to make, as long as you respect a few golden rules when you work the butter into the dough.

171

BRIOCHE

Brioche is the perfect bread for a Sunday morning breakfast and it works just as well as a base for desserts or French toast. If you do not have brioche molds at home, you can always use muffin molds instead.

20 BRIOCHES
5 cups (600 g) wheat flour
⅓ cup (60 g) granulated sugar *or* raw sugar
2 tsp (15 g) fleur de sel (fine sea salt)
12 cups (100 g) active floating sourdough
8–9 (1⅔ cups/400 g) eggs
9 oz (250 g) cold, unsalted butter
1 egg + a splash of water + a pinch of salt
   for glazing

DAY 1, EVENING *Thursday*

1. Mix flour, sugar, and salt on a baking table and make a dent in the middle. Add sourdough and egg to the dent and work in the flour mix until it turns to dough. Knead the dough for about 10 minutes or until it releases from the table.

2. Bang the butter with a rolling pin until flat and then work it into the dough a little bit at a time. Knead until you have a nice, smooth dough that releases from the table.

3. Let the dough rest at room temperature under a moist baking towel to let the leavening process begin. To ensure that the process has begun, make a small incision into the dough; if there are bubbles in the dough, the leavening process has begun. Wrap the dough in plastic wrap and let it rest in the fridge for 24 hours.

DAY 2, EVENING *Friday*

1. Divide the dough into 20 equal parts and shape them into small balls. Squeeze the dough balls with your thumb and index finger to give them a little round head (pg. 175). Grease twenty small molds and place the brioches in them. Glaze the brioches with a whisked egg, a splash of water, and a little bit of salt.

2. Place a pot of hot, boiling water on the bottom of the oven. In a cold oven, leaven the brioches overnight until they have doubled in size.

DAY 3, MORNING *Saturday*

1. Preheat the oven to 400°F (210°C).

2. Glaze the brioches one more time with egg, water, and salt.

3. Bake the brioches in the middle of the oven for 12 minutes.

4. Remove the brioches from the molds as soon as they are out of the oven and let them cool down on a rack.

BRIOCHE DE NANTERRE

Make ten little balls from the dough and let them leaven close to each other in a cake pan. You will now have a Brioche de Nanterre. If you can get a hold of praline roses (French sugary almonds), you can make a traditional Brioche de Saint Genix. Follow the above recipe but mix 1 cup (150 g) sugared almonds into the dough before leavening.

173

1. Grab the tip of the dough ball with your thumb and index finger. Squeeze until you have a round head.

2. It is important not to squeeze too hard or else the whole head may fall off.

3. If you squeeze too gently, the head may disappear during the baking.

4. Press on the edge to make sure the head ends up in the middle of the brioche.

LES CROISSANTS

Flaky on the outside, smooth and creamy on the inside with a subtle taste of hazelnut—a perfect croissant is judged by the mouth. If this is your first time making croissants, you're better off making the dough with yeast so that you can focus on the actual technique of creating them.

10–15 CROISSANTS

5 cups (600 g) wheat flour

⅓ cup (60 g) sugar

2 tsp (12 g) fleur de sel (fine sea salt)

1 small egg for the dough (1 oz/25 g) + 1 small egg for glazing

⅓ oz (10 g) fresh yeast *or* ½ cup (100 g) active sourdough

1⅓ cups (350 g/350 ml) milk

3½ tbsp (1¾ oz/50 g) unsalted butter for the dough

1⅓ cup (10½ oz/300 g) unsalted butter for the rolling of the dough

DAY 1, EVENING

1. Mix flour, sugar, and salt on a baking table. Make a dent in the middle of the flour and add the egg and sourdough or crumbled yeast. Pour milk into the dent, a little bit at a time, and work the flour into the mix until the dough becomes fairly dense. Let the dough rest under a baking towel at room temperature for 30–45 minutes.

2. Work 3½ tbsp (1¾ oz/50 g) of butter into the dough and knead for a couple of minutes.

3. Wrap the dough in plastic and let it rest for about 8 hours or overnight in the fridge.

DAY 2, MORNING

1. Pour the dough onto a baking table and roll it out into a rectangle until it is about ½ inch (1 cm) thick.

2. Bang on the cold butter with a floured rolling pin until it is about ½ inch (1 cm) thick. The butter should be about half as big as the dough by now.

3. Place the butter on top of the dough rectangle in the middle and fold the dough over the butter so it is completely covered (pg. 178–179).

4. Carefully roll out the dough lengthwise so it becomes even longer but is still a rectangle. Fold a quarter of the dough toward the middle. Then fold the other side toward the middle so the edges meet in the middle. Fold the dough in half so you get a fourfold. Wrap the dough in plastic and let it rest for 2 hours in the fridge.

5. Roll out the dough again and make another fourfold. Wrap the dough once more in plastic and let it rest in the fridge for 2 hours.

6. Roll out the dough on a floured baking table until it is 18 x 18 inches (45 x 45 cm) in size and is ⅛ inch (3–4 mm) thick.

7. Cut clean and even triangles out of the dough 5 x 5 x 5 inches (12 x 12 x 12 cm) and roll them up, starting at the wide edge and ending at the tip.

8. Place the croissants on a baking sheet covered with parchment paper and glaze them with an egg whisked with a splash of water and a pinch of salt.

9. Let the croissants leaven in a cold oven with a pot of hot water at the bottom. Remove your croissants when they have doubled in size. It should take about 2–4 hours if you use yeast and 10–12 hours if you are baking with sourdough.

10. Preheat the oven to 425°F (220°C).

11. Glaze the croissants one more time and bake them for 15–20 minutes or until they have turned a nice golden color. A well-baked croissant is the best thing there is, so it's better to bake them a few minutes longer than a few minutes short.

177

1. Roll out the dough until it is about ½ inch (1 cm) thick.

2. Bang out the cold butter with a rolling pin on a floured baking table.

3. Roll out the butter until it is a ½ inch (1 cm) thick rectangle. The butter should be about half as big as the dough.

4. Place the butter on top of the dough in the middle. Gently stretch the edges outwards.

5. Fold the edges over the butter and press down.

6. Fold the edges over on the short end so the butter is completely covered.

7. Carefully roll out the dough into a long rectangle.

8. Make a fourfold by folding a quarter of the dough toward the middle. Fold the other side of the dough toward the middle, so the two edges meet. Then fold the dough in half.

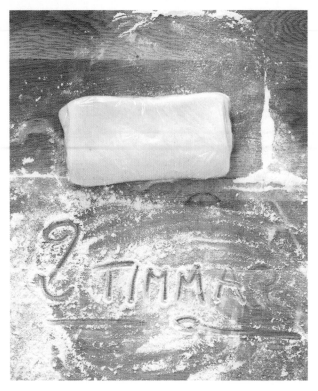

9. Brush off the flour from the dough with a brush. Wrap the dough in plastic and let it rest in the fridge for 2 hours.

10. Roll the dough into a long rectangle.

11. Make another fourfold. Brush off any flour with a brush.

12. Wrap the dough in plastic and let it rest in the fridge for 2 more hours.

13. Roll out the dough to 18 x 18 inches (45 x 45 cm).

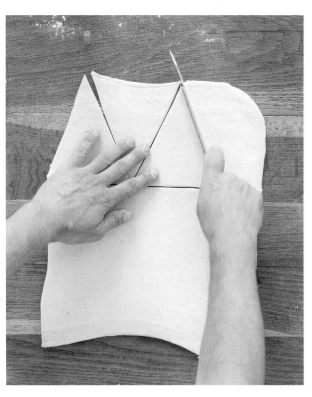

14. Cut out even triangles, 5 x 5 x 5 inches (12 x 12 x 12 cm).

15. Roll up the croissants from the wide edge to the tip. Glaze them and let leaven in a cold oven.

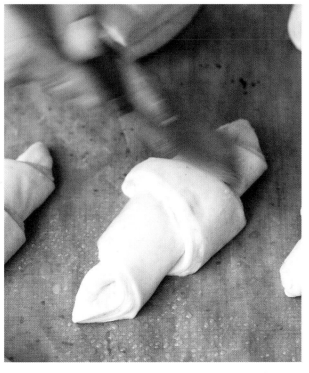

16. Glaze the croissants one more time before baking.

PAIN AU CHOCOLAT

When I lived and worked in the United States, my customers would call this pastry "pain in chocolate." It is a fairly accurate statement, since these are so painfully delicious. The quality of the chocolate is extremely important here. I use Valrhona dark chocolate, but you can make your own mix of, for example, milk chocolate and crushed hazelnuts. Just let your imagination run wild and create some memorable pains au chocolat.

15 PAINS AU CHOCOLAT

1 batch croissant dough, up until day 2, step 5 (pg. 177).

10 oz (300 g) high-quality dark chocolate, cut into small bars

1 egg + splash of water + a pinch of salt for glazing

DAY 1

1. Roll out the dough into a rectangle on a baking table sprinkled with flour until it is ⅛ inch (3–4 mm) thick.

2. Cut out ¼-inch (5–6 mm) wide strips from the dough (they should be as wide as the chocolate bars are long).

3. Place a chocolate bar at the top of each strip and fold a piece of the dough over it so it is covered (pg.186). Place another piece of chocolate on the dough and create another fold. Cut off any excess dough. It is important that the chocolate bars are placed next to each other instead of on top of each other when you have folded your pain au chocolat.

4. Place your pains au chocolat on a baking sheet covered with parchment paper and glaze them with a whisked egg mixed with a splash of water and a pinch of salt.

5. Let your pains au chocolat leaven in a cold oven until doubled in size. It should take 2–4 hours if you are using yeast and 10–12 hours if you use sourdough. You can also place a pot with boiling hot water at the bottom of the oven to get a really moist environment for the dough.

DAY 2

Glaze your pains au chocolat again. Bake in the oven at 425°F (220°C) for about 15 minutes or until they have turned golden brown and crispy.

Tip!
Raw, unleavened croissants and pains au chocolats can be frozen for 5–6 days. It's a good solution for Saturday morning croissants. You can have the prep work done ahead of time—all you have to do is take them out of the freezer on Friday night.

183

PAIN AUX RAISINS

Most people's favorite! I always roll the dough with plenty of vanilla cream in the middle to make the bread extra moist. Try using different kinds of raisins in the filling, such as currants or large, yellow sultan raisins. Don't forget to soak the raisins in water overnight—otherwise they might burn.

12–14 PAIN AUX RAISINS
1 batch croissant dough, up until day 2,
  step 4 (pg. 177)
2 cups (500 g/500 ml) water
¼ cup (50 g/50 ml) rum
⅓ cup (300 g) raisins, for example currants,
  sultan raisins, *or* regular
  raisins
1 batch crème pâtissière (pg. 234)
1 egg + a pinch of salt + a splash of water
  for glazing

SYRUP
1 cup (220 g) raw sugar
¾ cup (200 ml) water
1 vanilla bean

DAY 1, EVENING
Mix water, rum, and raisins in a bowl. Let soak at room temperature overnight.

DAY 2, MORNING
1. Roll out the croissant dough on a lightly floured baking table until it is ⅛ inch (3–4 mm) thick.
2. Whisk an egg, salt, and a splash of water and glaze slightly more than 1 inch (3 cm) of the bottom edge of the dough.
3. Spread out a layer of crème pâtissière over the dough, except for the glazed part.

4. Drain any excess water from the raisins. Spread them over the vanilla cream.
5. Fold about 2 inches (5 cm) of the upper long edge. Roll the dough from the top down. (The glazed part at the bottom functions as glue and helps keep the roll from opening during leavening and baking.)
6. Cut the roll into 2-inch (5–6 cm) wide slices and place them on a baking sheet covered with parchment paper. Make sure they are not too close together since they will leaven into twice their size.
7. Place the baking sheet in a cold oven and spray lightly with water to ensure the environment is moist. Leaven until doubled in size. This will take 2–4 hours if you have used yeast and 10–12 hours if you are using sourdough.
8. Remove the baking sheet and preheat the oven to 425°F (220°C).
9. *Making syrup:* Slice the vanilla bean open and scrape the seeds out into a pot. Add sugar, water, and vanilla bean. Bring to a boil. Remove the pot from the heat and pick out the vanilla bean.
10. Bake your pains aux raisins for 15–20 minutes. Glaze them immediately after bringing them out of the oven. They should be "singing" for you when you glaze them, otherwise it means that they are not hot enough and will end up sticky and soggy.

1. Place three chocolate bars at the top of the rolled out dough. Cut the dough into strips slightly thinner than the chocolate bars are wide.

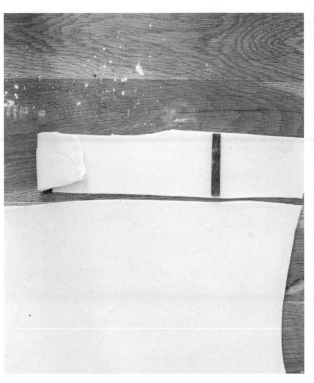

2. First place a chocolate bar about ½ inch (1 cm) from the left edge. Fold the dough over so the chocolate bar is completely covered.

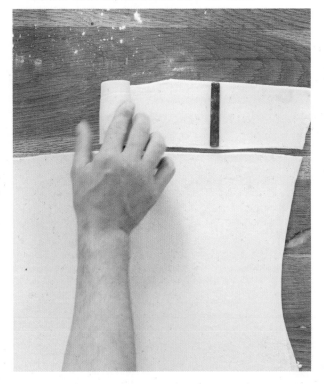

3. Place one chocolate bar on top of the fold and make another fold.

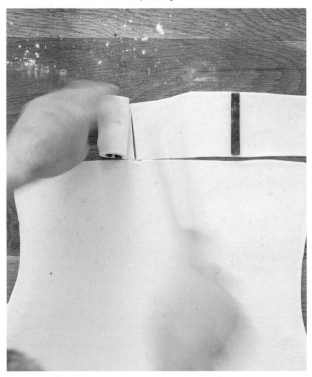

4. Cut off any excess dough and place your first pain aux chocolat on a baking sheet covered with parchment paper. Repeat procedure until all dough has been used up.

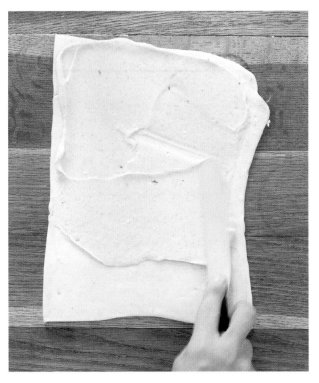

1. Spread out a layer of crème pâtissière over the rolled out dough. Leave a 1 inch (3 cm) edge at the bottom. Glaze the edge with a whisked egg.

2. Spread the raisins over the cream and roll the dough from the top down.

3. Cut the roll into 2 inch (5–6 cm) thick slices.

4. Place the pastry on a baking sheet covered with parchment paper. Make sure they are not too close together, since they will double in size when leavening.

CROISSANT AUX AMANDES

Reincarnate yesterday's croissants into lovely croissants aux amandes. In France, this pastry is often mistreated, baked from old, freezer-burned croissants and filled with overly sweet syrup and bad almond cream. A real almond croissant is a carefully baked piece of art from the countryside. The first time we served them at Petite France, they were an immediate success. Almond flour can be found at specialty grocery stores or food markets.

12 ALMOND CROISSANTS
12 one-day-old croissants (pg. 177)

ALMOND CREAM
¾ cup (150 g) sugar
5 oz (150 g) soft butter
1½ cups (150 g) almond flour
3 (5 oz/150 g) eggs
3 tbsp (20 g) wheat flour

SYRUP
1 cup (220 g) raw sugar
¾ cup (200 ml) water
1 vanilla bean

7 oz (200 g) sliced almonds
powdered sugar

1. Mix the sugar and butter for the almond cream until you get a smooth consistency.
2. Add the almond flour, a little bit at a time, and stir until consistency is smooth.
3. Add the eggs, one at a time. Each egg should be completely worked into the cream before adding the next.

4. Sift the flour into the mix and stir carefully.
5. Cover the bowl with plastic. It's vital that it is sealed airtight. Let the bowl rest in the fridge for 2–3 hours.
6. Preheat the oven to 400°F (200°C).
7. *Making syrup:* Slice the vanilla bean open and scrape the seeds out into a pot. Add sugar, water, and vanilla bean. Bring to a boil. Remove the pot from the burner and remove the vanilla bean.
8. Cut the old croissants lengthwise and glaze them on top and bottom with the syrup.
9. Spread some almond cream on the bottom part and place the "lid" on top.
10. Spread some almond cream on top of the "lid" and sprinkle with sliced almonds.
11. Place the almond croissants on a baking sheet covered with parchment paper and bake them in the oven for 15–20 minutes or until they are golden brown.
12. Remove the croissants from the oven and let them cool down on a rack. Sprinkle powdered sugar on top before serving.

LE CINNAMON ROLL

My darling! A rustic, simple, everyday bun that deserves great respect. As time equals more flavor, these cinnamon rolls are made from sourdough, as its flavor develops with time. And it doesn't leave you with stomach pains!

15 CINNAMON ROLLS
5½ cups (700 g) wheat flour
½ cup (100 g) raw sugar
1½ tsp (10 g) salt
3 tsp (10 g) coarsely ground cardamom
1 (2 oz/50 g) egg
1½ cups (150 g/350 ml) milk
½ cup (80 g) active sourdough
7 tbsp (3½ oz/100 g) soft butter

FILLING
14 tbsp (7 oz/200 g) soft butter
3 oz (80 g) sugar
6 tsp cinnamon

pearl sugar for garnish

DAY 1

1. In a pot, melt half the butter for the filling (do not boil). Remove from the heat and stir in the sugar and cinnamon. Add the rest of the butter and whisk until the consistency is smooth. Cover the filling with plastic wrap and store at room temperature.

2. Mix flour, sugar, salt, and cardamom on a table and make a dent in the middle.

3. Pour egg, milk, and sourdough into the dent and mix until the dough is smooth.

4. Knead the dough until it releases from the table. Let the dough rest for 20 minutes under a baking towel.

5. Add the butter, a little bit at a time, by squeezing it into the dough. Let the dough rest at room temperature under a moist baking towel for 2 hours.

6. Wrap the dough in plastic and let it rest in the fridge for another hour.

7. Roll the dough out to a ⅛ inch (3–4 mm) square. Fold over a third of the dough toward the middle of the square, and then take the rest of the dough on the opposite side and fold it over as well—you should have a three layer dough. Cut strips lengthwise that are 1 inch (2 cm) wide. Stretch the dough gently lengthwise. Twist the dough two and a half times around your index and middle finger and then cross the edge over the bun and fold it in. Secure the edge at the bottom.

8. Place the rolls on a baking sheet covered with parchment paper and spray them with water. Leaven the rolls in a cold oven until doubled in size—about 8–12 hours. To ensure a moist environment, place a pot of boiling hot water at the bottom of the oven.

DAY 2

1. Preheat the oven to 400°F (200°C).

2. Spray the rolls or glaze them with water and sprinkle pearl sugar on top. Bake them in the middle of the oven for 10–14 minutes or until they have a nice golden color. Let the rolls cool down on a rack under a baking towel.

LE CHAUSSON AUX POMMES

Wonderful puff pastry pockets filled with apples! Le chausson aux pommes means "apple slipper," and with a little bit of imagination, you can actually see the tip of a slipper. I add more apples at the end of the process to create a varied texture. Be sure to start preparing the puff pastry two days ahead of time.

12 PUFF PASTRY POCKETS
1 batch puff pastry (pg. 194)

APPLE COMPOTE
8 cored and chopped apples
2 cups (500 g/500 ml) water
4½ tbsp (2⅓ oz/65 g) butter
1½ oz (40 g) sugar

SYRUP
⅓ cup (100 ml) water
4 oz (120 g) sugar

1 egg + a pinch of salt + a splash of water
for glazing

DAY 1

1. Boil water and sugar into syrup. Let it cool down and store in the fridge.
2. Prepare the apple compote by boiling half the apple chunks with the sugar and half the water. Let it simmer over low heat for about 30 minutes—keep the lid on the pot.
3. Add another cup (250 g) water and the rest of the apple chunks and let it simmer for another 15 minutes with closed lid.
4. Remove the pot from the burner and add the butter. Stir until the butter has melted.
5. Let the apple compote cool. Then place it in the fridge overnight.

DAY 2

1. Roll out the dough on a floured baking table until it is about an ⅛ of an inch (3 mm) thick.
2. Cut out 12 oval pieces from the dough.
3. Whisk the egg, a pinch of salt, and a splash of water for glazing. Glaze the bottom part of the puff pastry and spread out the apple compote in the middle of the dough.
4. Fold over one half of the puff pastry and press down hard with your fingertips.
5. Place your chaussons upside down on a baking sheet covered with parchment paper and glaze with egg mixture.
6. Score decorative designs into the top and bottom of the pastry with a knife. You can make any pattern you like—be as creative as you want. The most important thing is to remember not to cut too deeply into the dough. You don't want the apple compote to leak out.
7. Let the puff pastry pockets rest in the fridge for 1 hour.
8. Preheat the oven to 450°F (230°C).
9. Glaze the pockets with the rest of the whisked egg and bake for 25 minutes in the middle of the oven.
10. Glaze your chaussons with cold sugar syrup as soon as you take them out of the oven. They should "sing" when you glaze them. If they don't, they are not hot enough.

193

SHORTCRUST PASTRY & PUFF PASTRY

Two indispensible recipes that can be made ahead of time and stored in the freezer until you need them. Before baking with the dough, it is important to always let it thaw for 24 hours after taking it out of the freezer.

SHORTCRUST PASTRY

7 tbsp (3½ oz/100 g) cold butter
1½ cup (200 g) wheat flour
1 tsp (5 g) fleur de sel (fine sea salt)
½ cup (100 g) sugar
1 (1½ oz/40 g) egg

DAY 1

1. Sift the cold butter with flour, salt, and sugar between your hands until it reaches a grainy consistency. It is important for it not to have a doughy consistency yet.
2. Add the egg and mix until the dough is compact. Wrap the dough in plastic and let it rest in the fridge for 12 hours.

DAY 2

Remove the dough from the fridge and place it on a floured baking table. Knead thoroughly until the dough is smooth and even. To check if the dough is ready, take a small piece and roll it into a ball. Press a finger into it. If the edges do not crack, the dough has the right elasticity. Wrap the dough in plastic and let it rest in the fridge for at least 1 hour.

PUFF PASTRY

1 cup (9 oz/250 g) unsalted softened butter
¾ cup (100 g) wheat flour

5¼ tbsp (2½ oz/75 g) unsalted softened butter
2 cups (250 g) wheat flour
¼ cup (60 g) water
1 tsp (8 g) fleur de sel (fine sea salt)
1 tsp white wine vinegar

DAY 1

1. Mix 1 cup (9 oz/250 g) butter and ¾ cup (100 g) flour with a wooden spoon until it has turned to dough. Shape the dough into a flat square. Wrap it in plastic and let it rest in the fridge for 12 hours.
2. Quickly mix in the rest of the ingredients with a wooden spoon until it turns to dough. Don't overwork it. Shape the dough into a flat square, the same size as the first one. Wrap the dough in plastic and let it rest in the fridge for 12 hours.

DAY 2

1. Place the first square on a floured baking table and place the second square on top. Roll them lengthwise until they have merged into one puff pastry square.

2. When the puff pastry is three times as long as it is wide, make a threefold: fold over a third of the dough toward the middle and then fold the other side over. Turn the dough 90 degrees, roll out the dough, and make another threefold. Wrap it in plastic and let it rest in the fridge for 2 hours.

3. Remove the dough from the fridge, roll it out lengthwise, and make another threefold. Turn the dough 90 degrees and repeat. Wrap the dough in plastic once more and let it rest in the fridge for 12 hours. By then, the dough is ready to bake with or to frozen and used at a later date.

Petite France

A Little Piece of France

Petite France is like one of my children. What began as a declaration of love to my profession and my home country has grown into what it is today: a meeting place with a French soul—one where everyone is welcome. It is a bakery, a café, and a restaurant all under one roof, where each part is of equal importance.

The year was 2004 and I had just started the little sourdough bakery Petite France at Stora Essingen in Stockholm. I had left my job as a pastry chef at Berns and we had found a great space, which we rebuilt into one of Stockholm's first bakeries to deliver sourdough bread.

In the beginning, I had to fight to have my sourdough bread served at the finer hotel breakfast buffets in Stockholm. I was told that the crust was too thick and the bread too hard to chew. But after hiding for a while behind spongy, industrial breads, my bread started getting more space on the tables. Four years later, almost all industrially made bread has vanished from those buffets.

It was amazing to watch more than three hundred pounds (1500 kg) of sourdough bread being delivered to every corner of the city each morning. But at the same time, I felt that something was missing: a storefront and a window to the world. The hunt for new space began and soon I found a corner bistro, Restaurant Salzer on John Ericssongatan. After doing some research, I found out that the location of the restaurant had an amazing history. It was the spot of Sweden's first collective housing and the architect was none other than the famous Sven Markelius, with assistance from Alva Myrdal.

If you lived on John Ericssongatan in the '30s, you would have access to daycare; a dining hall where you could have your breakfast, lunch, and dinner; a dairy boutique; and a cleaning lady. In addition to this, there was a laundry drop off, where you could just throw your dirty clothes and have them returned to you, clean, later on. In the building I was considering for Petite France, was a dumbwaiter that provided residents with food from the kitchen located on the bottom floor. A house and a piece of Swedish history that—due to its dedicated board members—has been preserved up until today.

I fell in love with everything from the architecture to the corner location. on Kungsholmen. I wanted my Petite France to be a place passersby just happened upon. Today, many people have happened upon it, but the greatest part of all is that the dream of a Petite France where everyone is welcome has come to life.

Petite France has now been sold, or rather, has been adopted. A place called Petite France is a place that needs time, love, and dedication. Unfortunately, I did not have enough time to be able to continue giving it all the attention it needed. But even though I have other dreams to pursue and bring into reality, there will always be a part of my heart left at John Ericssongatan 6.

197

Picardy is home to one of France's finest cities, Gerberoy. The city is like one big garden, with roses blooming everywhere.

7 PETITS COOKIES

In French, these cookies are called gateaux de voyage—cookies to travel with. At our house, we bake all the time, and my children and I are true cookie monsters. Each child has his own cookie jar, which they refill with the cookies they bake during the week. I don't know how to describe the happiness and pride that light up their faces when they place the jars on the breakfast table each weekend.

201

FINANCIER

A delicate cookie made from egg whites and almond flour, baked on a small baking sheet with a slanted edge. I always have plenty of egg whites in the fridge and sometimes, when I'm not in the mood to bake macaroons or if I want to go with something simple, these cookies are perfect. They aren't sticky, nor do they crumble; they feel luxurious, but are not too much, and are therefore suitable for all occasions. Try substituting the almond flour for pistachio or cashew flour and then sprinkle the cookies with the same nuts as the flour you are using.

25 COOKIES
2½ cups (280 g) powdered sugar
2 cups (190 g) almond flour
¾ cup (90 g) wheat flour
9 (9½ oz/270 g) eggs
¾ cup (7 oz/190 g) butter

1. Preheat the oven to 355°F (180°C).
2. Sift powdered sugar, almond flour, and wheat flour into a bowl. Stir in the egg whites until the mixture is smooth in texture.
3. Melt the butter while stirring constantly until it has reached a nice, golden brown color. Add the melted butter to the mixture, a little bit at a time, while stirring constantly.
4. Divide the batter into 25 small cookie molds, with the batter almost reaching all the way up to the top of them. Sprinkle some nuts on top.
5. Bake the cookies for about 12 minutes in the middle of the oven.
6. Remove the cookies from the molds and let them cool on a rack.

LANGUE DE CHAT (CAT TONGUE)

A favorite of the royal court during the 1700–1800s. Perhaps because it doesn't crumble, leaving guests with cookie crumbs in their laps? The cookie requires a certain coordination and can be a little bit tricky to make, but it's well worth the time and effort.

50 COOKIES
1 vanilla bean
¾ cup (7 oz/190 g) butter
1⅓ cups (150 g) wheat flour
1¾ cups (210 g) powdered sugar
6–7 (7 oz/200 g) eggs

DAY 1

1. Score the vanilla bean lengthwise and scrape out the seeds into a pot. Melt the butter with the seeds. Remove the pot from the burner and let the butter cool.

2. Sift flour and powdered sugar into a bowl. Stir the egg whites into the mix by using a spatula. Pour in most of the butter, a little bit at a time, by holding the spatula in your right hand and holding the bowl with the left hand (if you are left-handed, do the opposite). At the same time as you stir, rotate the bowl in the opposite direction. It is important to have the spatula reach all the way down in the bowl and to turn the batter over so the bottom reaches the top. Repeat the process until you have turned all the batter over. Cover with plastic wrap and let it sit in the fridge overnight.

DAY 2

1. Preheat the oven to 400°F (200°C).

2. Pour the batter into a pastry bag with a ¼-inch (5 mm) wide tip and pipe the dough into 2-inch (5 cm) long "sausages" on a greased baking sheet. Bake in the oven for about 5-6 minutes or until the edges have a golden brown color.

LES NONETTES

A trusty little cookie filled with orange jam. It was traditionally baked by nuns. A lot of honey and rye flour make this cookie both nutritious and delicious.

10 COOKIES
⅔ cup (5¼ oz/150 g) unsalted butter
¾ cup (200 g/200 ml) orange juice
the rind from 1 orange
1 tsp (5 g) ground cinnamon
½ tsp (3 g) ground cardamom
10 oz (275 g) honey
1 cup (100 g) finely ground rye flour
2 cups (200 g) wheat flour
3½ tsp (12 g) baking powder
½ cup (150 g) orange jam
½ cup (50 g) powdered sugar
¼ cup (50 g/50 ml) orange juice (optional)

1. Melt the butter with the orange juice, zest, cinnamon, and cardamom on low heat. Remove the pot from the burner and add the honey. Let the mixture cool.

2. Sift flour and baking powder into a bowl. Add the cooled butter mixture and stir with a spatula until you have a smooth batter without any lumps. Cover the bowl with plastic wrap and let it rest in the fridge for 1 hour.

3. Preheat the oven to 400°F (200°C).

4. Pour the batter into small muffin molds and bake for 15 minutes in the middle of the oven.

5. Pipe the orange jam into the middle of the cookies as soon as they come out of the oven (If you prefer, you can even pipe the jam before you bake them.)

6. Mix orange juice and powdered sugar and glaze the cookies while they are still warm. Or omit the orange juice and simply roll the cookies in the powdered sugar.

SABLÉ BRETON

These are the pride of Bretagne and a part of French cultural heritage. In Bretagne, you will find the best salt and the best butter, and in this simple but delicious cookie, the butter and the salt play the lead roles. Bake them at low temperatures so the cookies will rise slowly and their core will stay moist.

30 COOKIES
4 (3 oz/80 g) egg yolks
1 cup (160 g) sugar
1¾ cups (225 g) wheat flour
4 tsp (15 g) baking powder
1 cup (7½ oz/210 g) softened butter
1 tsp (3 g) fleur de sel

DAY 1

1. Whisk the egg yolks and sugar into a fluffy, white batter.
2. Sift together the flour and baking powder, and then use a spatula to fold the mixture into the egg batter. The dough should become dry and crumbly.
3. Knead the butter into the dough and add the salt. Sprinkle some flour onto the dough and wrap it in plastic. Place it in the fridge and let it rest for 24 hours.

DAY 2

1. Preheat the oven to 285°F (140°C).
2. Divide the dough into 30 small balls. Place the balls into silicone molds about ⅓ cup (100 ml) in size. Press down with your thumb to flatten the surfaces.
3. Bake the cookies in the middle of the oven for 20–25 minutes or until they turn golden yellow. Remove the cookies from the molds and let them cool on a rack. Store them in a metal container with a tight sealing lid and they will stay fresh for weeks.

Tip! You can also press the Sablé Breton dough into a pie pan and bake it at 285°F (140°C) for 40–45 minutes. Remove the pan from the oven and press hard on top of the pie with the bottom of a plastic bowl or something similar. Pipe with vanilla cream and decorate with fresh berries. It's the simplest and most delicious pie you can make!

CHOUQUETTE

There is one kind of pastry I have always made as a baker: small chouquettes. I do not know how many millions of times I have piped cookies or how many millions of times I have had to explain what chouquettes are. My answer is always the same: a small pastry filled with French air! A perfect chouquette is fluffy, crispy, and flaky with a caramelized bottom and an interior flavor that reminds you of delicate pancakes.

50 COOKIES
2½ cups (300 g) wheat flour
1 cup (250 g/250 ml) water
1 cup (250 g/250 ml) milk
1⅔ tsp (5 g) fleur de sel (fine sea salt)
1⅔ tsp (5 g) sugar
1 cup (9 oz/250 g) unsalted butter
8–10 (17½ oz/500 g) eggs
pearl sugar for decorating

1. Turn on the oven at 410°F (210°C).
2. Sift the flour over parchment paper or into a bowl.
3. Heat the water, milk, salt, sugar, and butter over low heat. Remove the pot from the burner just as it starts to bubble.
4. Pour the flour into the mix and stir forcibly with a wooden spoon. Return the pot to the burner and continue to stir until the batter releases from the edges and becomes a dry, compact, shiny mass. The batter is ready when it releases from the wooden spoon without leaving any trace behind. Remove the pot from the burner and tip the batter over into a clean bowl.
5. Add the eggs, one at a time, into the warm batter while stirring forcibly. It is important that each egg is worked well into the batter before adding another one. Since the weight of eggs can vary greatly (sometimes 8 eggs are enough, sometimes you will need 10), it is important to get to know the batter to understand what it's supposed to look and feel like. The batter is supposed to be slow-moving; when it drips from the spoon into a beak-like shape, it has the right consistency.
6. Pour the batter into a pastry bag with a small tip (to ensure that the batter will not dry up in between piping, just cover it with a moist towel) and pipe small balls onto parchment paper. Since the chouquettes will expand up to three times their size, it is important not to pipe them too close together.
7. Sprinkle plenty of pearl sugar on top and bake for 20–25 minutes in the middle of the oven. Note: Do not open the oven door during the baking process—the chouquettes will deflate if you do. They are ready when they have a golden color but are still somewhat white at the edges.

Tip! If you prefer a savory version, omit the pearl sugar and sprinkle some cheese on top before the baking. Split the chouquettes just before serving and fill them with a layer of cream cheese.

Mes enfants

The apple never falls far from the tree.

As the saying goes; the apple never falls far from the tree (in French, the saying is "dogs do not make cats"). My three children—Oliver, Antoine, and Hugo—love to bake. I think the children bake more than anyone else in the house! Sourdough bread, cookies, buns, and brioches, and preferably several at a time. Our kitchen often looks like a war zone: dirty dishes everywhere and dough stuck on the walls—and sometimes even on the ceiling! But the energy is high and I am impressed and proud of how good they really are, as individuals and as a team. It's great fun to watch them bake, and I have to bite my tongue many times to make sure I do not interfere. Our pantry at home only contains ingredients without any additives. NO SHAKE AND BAKE! All my children know this and we work together to clean out the pantry. (Yes, we too have times when we need to clean out things that don't belong there.) The first thing they do when we buy a new kind of product is read through the list of nutritional facts. But the most important thing for me is that my children are finding pleasure and joy in baking at the same time they succeed in their goals without taking any shortcuts. Many children don't seem to understand what it takes to build something from the ground up, nor do they comprehend the importance of letting time take its course. Not everything can be ready immediately just because you want it to be. Today, so many things are about instant gratification—like a quick adrenaline kick that disappears after only a few minutes. It worries me and makes me sad when I think about how many children today are missing out on the opportunity of feeling true longing for something. In my world, longing is the main ingredient of pleasure. When something takes time, we get a chance to long for it, and in the end, everything tastes so much better. The evening pancakes are so much more delicious when they were planned

Oliver, Antoine, Hugo, and me in the middle of making dough knots to create our cinnamon rolls.

214

Le gateau au chocolat

- Allumer le four à 175°C.
- Battre 250g d'œufs (4-5 st) avec 200g de sucre.
- Faire fondre 150g de chocolat au lait dans un bain-marie.
- Faire fondre 100g de beurre doux au micro-onde.
- Tamiser ensemble 120g de farine, 7g de levure chimique, 90g de poudre d'amande et 25g de cacao.
- bien fouetter et faire disparaître les grumeaux.
- Verser sur la pâte 120g de crème fouettée et le beurre fondu.
- Bien mélanger avec une maryse jusqu'à l'obtention d'une pâte homogène.
- Mettre la pâte dans un moule beurré et cuire pendant ~~enf~~ environ 45-50 minutes.

Oliver has his own recipe book, where he writes down his recipes in French (with some minor spelling errors—just like Dad).

and prepared the day before—not just because the flavors get a chance to develop, but rather because our longing for it adds that special flavor to the food. If Oliver, Antoine, or Hugo would ask me at 5 p.m. one afternoon if we can make pancakes for dinner, my answer would be, "No, unfortunately that's not possible. You should have planned better and made the batter yesterday. You can have pancakes tomorrow if you want to prepare the batter, but then you have to make it right now so it has the chance to rest overnight." In the meantime, I'll make a large omelet with cheese for dinner and the children can long for the pancakes of tomorrow. Because good food and good bread definitely are about three things: ingredients, time, and longing.

MADELEINE COOKIES

With its little point rising in the middle, it almost looks like a boat. As children, my brothers and I put our Madeleine cookies in a bowl of milk and whoever's cookie sank the fastest lost the competition. If you don't have a Madeleine baking pan, you can always use some well cleaned scallop shells.

20 COOKIES
¾ cup (6 oz/170 g) butter
1⅔ cups (210 g) wheat flour
2 tsp (8 g) baking powder
1 vanilla bean
3 (5 oz/150 g) eggs
1 cup (170 g) sugar
the zest of ½ a lemon

1. Preheat the oven to 425°F (220°C).
2. Melt the butter over low heat while stirring. Remove the pot from the burner and let it cool.
3. Sift the flour and baking powder into a bowl. Score the vanilla bean lengthwise and scrape out the seeds.
4. Carefully mix vanilla seeds, eggs, and sugar in a bowl. Add the flour mix and stir with a spatula.

5. Add the butter mix, a little bit at a time, while stirring with a spatula, holding the bowl with your left hand and stirring with your right (if you are left-handed, do the opposite). Rotate the bowl while stirring in the opposite direction. The spatula should reach all the way to the bottom of the bowl so you can turn the batter over completely as you stir. Continue stirring until the batter is completely smooth.
6. Add the lemon zest to the mix.
7. Pipe the batter into the Madeleine molds, filling them almost to the rim. The cookies will expand during baking so make sure not to fill them completely.
8. Reduce the heat in the oven to 400°F (200°C) and bake the cookies for 7–9 minutes in the middle of the oven. Remove the cookies from the molds and let them cool on a rack.

"No sooner had the warm liquid, and the [Madeleine] crumbs with it, touched my palate than a shudder ran through my whole body, and I stopped, intent upon the extraordinary changes that were taking place. An exquisite pleasure had invaded my senses . . . Whence could it have come to me, this all-powerful joy?"

Marcel Proust, *In Search of Lost Time*

LE CANNELÉ

A real pearl from Bourdeaux, with a crispy surface and a soft and creamy interior. Don't hold back on the vanilla and the rum—you'll only regret it later. The most important thing in this recipe is to make sure not to get any air into the batter. The air will result in a hollow interior and a cookie that will rise too high in the oven, only to deflate when it comes out.

12 COOKIES
2 vanilla beans
1¾ tsbp (1 oz/25 g) butter
1⅔ cups (400 g/400 ml) milk
a pinch of fleur de sel (fine sea salt)
⅔ oz (20 g) egg yolk
1 (1½ oz/50 g) egg
⅔ cup (150 g) sugar
½ cup (60 g) wheat flour
5 tsbp high-quality rum
melted butter for glazing

DAY 1

1. Score the vanilla beans lengthwise and scrape the seeds into a pot. Melt the butter with the vanilla seeds, milk, and a pinch of salt over low heat until it is close to a boil.
2. Add egg yolk, egg, and sugar and mix with a hand mixer. Note: It is important that no air gets into the batter.
3. Sift the flour and add it into the egg mixture while you continue to mix.
4. Carefully add the butter mix while stirring with a spatula. Add some rum for flavor.
5. Cover the bowl with plastic wrap and let the batter rest overnight in the fridge.

DAY 2

1. Preheat the oven to 355°F (180°C).
2. Carefully stir the batter with a spatula to make sure vanilla seeds have not settled on the bottom of the bowl.
3. Grease the cannelé molds with some melted butter and divide the batter into the molds. Bake them in the middle of the oven for 45 minutes.
4. Tip the cookies onto a rack right after they come out of the oven and let them cool.

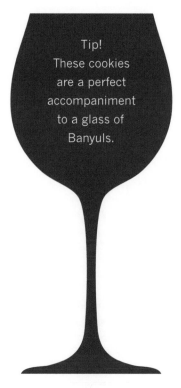

Tip!
These cookies
are a perfect
accompaniment
to a glass of
Banyuls.

218

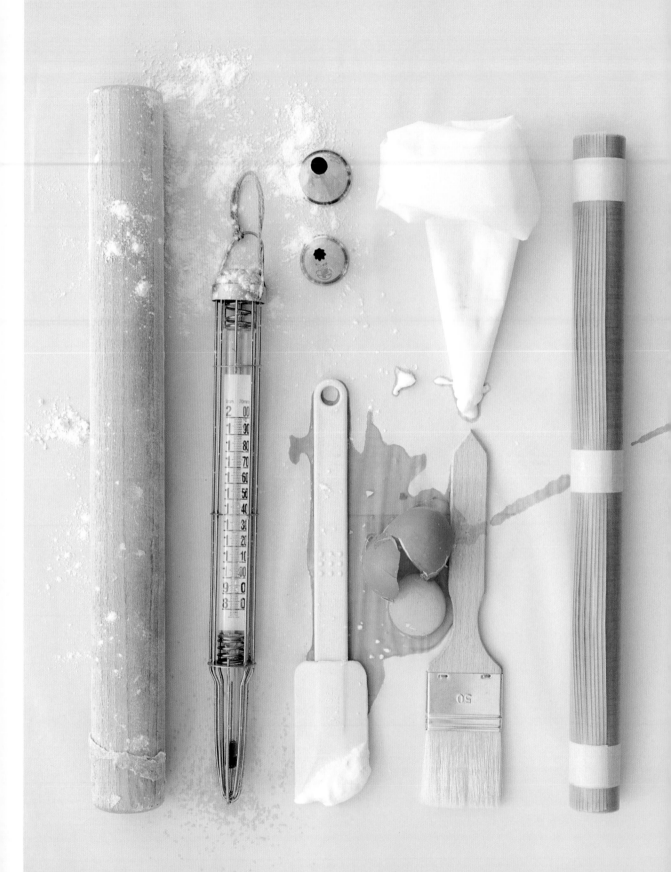

LES DESSERTS

I am a pastry chef first and foremost. I have baked all sorts of pastries and cakes all around the world, both in bakeries and in restaurants. For a long time, my life was completely dedicated to sweet delicacies—until I discovered the magic of sourdough. Since desserts are still close to my heart, I have included some real French classics in this book. These will finish off your dinners in the most wonderful ways.

221

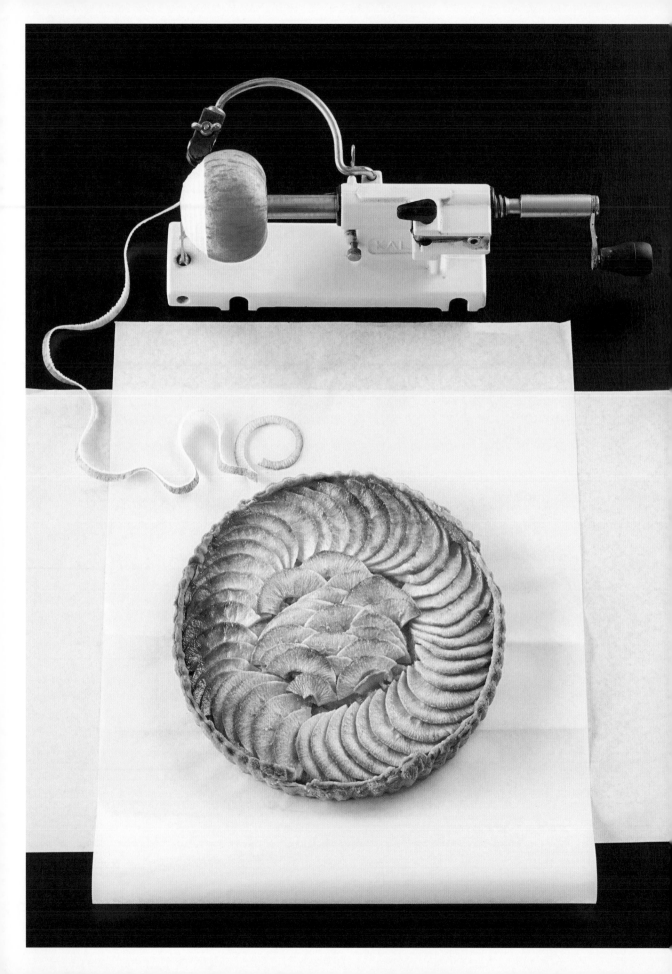

FRENCH APPLE PIE

The French apple pie, with its delicate apple slices, is an homage to the pie itself. The focus is on respect for its ingredients. It is supposed to taste like apple and butter. No crumbs, nothing clever, nothing fluffy, no tricks!

PIE CRUST, 8–10 PORTIONS
7 tbsp (3½ oz/100 g) cold butter
1¾ cups (200 g) wheat flour
a pinch of fleur de sel (fine sea salt)
½ cup (100 g) sugar
1 (1½ oz/40 g) small egg

APPLE COMPOTE
6 apples + 4 apples
1 lemon
1 cup (200–300 g/200–300 ml) water
1 vanilla bean

1½ cups (400 g) almond cream at room
     temperature
raw sugar for the pan

DAY 1
1. Sift the cold butter between your hands with the flour, sugar, and salt until you have a coarse consistency. It's important that it not yet turn into dough.
2. Add the egg and mix until you have a compact dough. Wrap the dough in plastic and let it rest in the fridge for 12 hours.

DAY 2
1. Remove the dough from the fridge and place it on a baking table sprinkled with flour. Let it rest at room temperature for 15 minutes. Knead until the dough is nice and smooth. To check if the dough is ready, you can take a piece and shape it into a ball. Press with your finger into it—if the edges are not cracking and the dough stays elastic, it is ready. Wrap the dough and place it in the fridge for about 1 hour.
2. Peel, core, and cut the apples into small chunks. Place them in a pot.
3. Score the vanilla bean and scrape out the seeds into the pot of apple chunks.
4. Add water, the zest from one lemon, and the juice from half a lemon. Bring to a boil and then let it simmer over low heat. Stir once in a while to make sure it does not burn. Pour the compote into a bowl and cover it with plastic wrap. (It is important that the plastic wrap is in direct contact with the compote, creating an airtight environment.)
5. Preheat the oven to 400°F (200°C).
6. Grease a pie pan and sprinkle some raw sugar to get a crispier exterior.
7. Roll out the dough so that it's flat and round and place it in the pie pan. Press the dough toward the edges of the pan with your hands.
8. Fill a pastry bag with the almond cream. Pipe the cream in circles onto the pie crust, starting in the middle and working your way out.
9. Bake the pie for 25 minutes in the middle of the oven. Remove the pie and reduce the heat to 355°F (180°C).
10. Spread the apple compote on top of the crust. Peel and core the rest of the apples and slice them thinly. Place the apple slices on top of the compote in an overlapping, circular design. Bake in the middle of the oven for another 50 minutes.

223

SAVARIN

This is a cousin to the brioche. Fluffy, porous, and exploding with raisins or currants. This cake got its name from Jean Anthelme Brillat-Savarin—an attorney, politician, and gastronome from the 1700s who once said, "Le plasir de manger est le seul qui, pris avec modération, ne soit pas suivi de fatigue." ("The pleasure of eating, when done in moderation, is the only act that is not followed by tiredness.")

8 PORTIONS

1⅔ oz (50 g/50 ml) tepid milk

⅕ oz (5 g) yeast

¼ cup (50 g) + 1½ cup (175 g) wheat flour

3 (3 oz/150 g) eggs

1 tsp (5 g) salt

1¾ oz cold, unsalted butter

melted butter for greasing the savarin molds

¾ oz raisins or currants

SYRUP

2 cups (500 g/500 ml) water

1½ cup (300 g) raw sugar

1 vanilla bean

zest from 1 orange

zest from 1 lemon

10 whole Sichuan peppercorns

1 cup (200 g/200 ml) dark rum

1 batch crème pâtissière (pg. 234)

fresh, seasonal fruit and berries

1. Mix milk, yeast, and ¼ cup (50 g) flour in a stainless steel bowl. Stir for 2–3 minutes with a wooden spoon. Cover the bowl with a moist towel and let it leaven for 2–3 hours or until doubled in size.

2. Mix together the rest of the flour, eggs, and salt with a mixer (with a blade attachment) on the lowest speed, until the dough releases from the edges.

3. Bang out the cold butter with a rolling pin and then work it into the dough.

4. Add the raisins or currants and stir until they are evenly distributed. Let the dough rest for a few minutes.

5. Grease the savarin molds (¾ cup cylinder-shaped molds with smooth edges) with some melted butter.

6. Dollop a spoonful of dough into each mold. It is important to distribute the dough evenly and to make sure that the molds are no more than a third full.

7. Cover the molds with a moist baking towel and let them leaven for 1–3 hours or until the cakes have risen close enough to the edges of the molds.

8. Preheat the oven to 355°F (180°C).

9. *Making the syrup:* Bring all ingredients to a boil and let simmer for a few minutes. Remove the pot from the heat and cover it with plastic wrap. Let the syrup rest for 30 minutes and then strain the spices from the mixture.

10. Bake the savarins for 25–30 minutes in the middle of the oven. Remove them from the molds as soon as they are taken out of the oven. Let them cool on a rack.

11. Cut the savarins lengthwise and pour the syrup over them. Let them soak up the syrup until time to serve.

12. Place your savarins on a plate and pour the rum over them just before serving. Pipe a dollop of crème pâtissière and garnish with fresh fruits and berries.

RASPBERRY TART

Raspberries always taste their best when they are really fresh. Feel free to replace them with other fruits and berries according to the season.

12 TARTS

TART CRUST

7 tbsp (3½ oz/100 g) cold butter
1⅔ cups (200 g) wheat flour
½ cup (100 g) sugar
a pinch of fleur de sel (fine sea salt)
1 (1½ oz/40 g) egg

GELATIN

½ vanilla bean
1 cup (250 g/250 ml) cold water
zest and juice from ½ orange
zest and juice from ½ lemon
1 cup (225 g) jam sugar
5 fresh mint leaves
5 black peppercorns

1 batch almond cream (pg. 189)
1 batch crème pâtissière (pg. 234)
6 cups (750 g) fresh raspberries
shredded lemon rind for garnishing (optional)

DAY 1

1. Sift the cold butter between your hands with flour, sugar, and salt until you get a grainy consistency. Make sure it has not yet turned into dough.
2. Add the egg and mix into a compact dough. Wrap the dough in plastic and let it rest in the fridge for 12 hours.

DAY 2

1. Remove the dough from the fridge and let it rest on a floured baking table at room temperature for about 15 minutes.

2. Thoroughly knead the dough with your hands until it becomes nice and smooth. Check that it is ready by taking a piece and pressing your finger into it—if the edges do not crack, it is ready. Wrap the dough in plastic and put it back into the fridge until it is cold again.
3. *Preparing the gelatin:* Score the vanilla bean lengthwise and scrape out all the seeds into a pot. Include the bean as well. Mix all other ingredients (it is important that they are all cold) and bring to a boil. Remove the pot from the burner, cover with a lid, and let rest for 30 minutes. Sift the mixture to remove the spices. Cover the pot with plastic and place it somewhere cold.
4. Preheat the oven to 355°F (180°C).
5. Roll out the dough and cut out small, round shapes to fit into your tart molds.
6. Bake the tart crusts in the middle of the oven for 10 minutes and then increase the heat to 400°F (200°C).
7. Remove the tart crusts from the molds and pipe some almond cream into each crust. Bake for another 10–12 minutes. Let them cool down.
8. Whisk the crème pâtissière until all lumps are gone and the cream is smooth and silky. Pipe the cream into the crusts and decorate with raspberries on top of each tart.
9. Heat the gelatin until it turns to liquid. Use this to glaze the berries to give them a nice sheen and a lovely taste. Garnish with shredded lemon rind, if you like.

Damien

The Engineer Who Became a Pastry Chef and Vice Versa

Damien is not a typical baby brother. As a child, he was not treated the way most babies of the family are, and you can tell that he really had to work hard for everything he has. He came to Sweden a few years ago to study and finally fulfilled our parents' dream of having an engineer in the family. Unfortunately, both my brother, Marc, and I had crushed our parents' hopes the day we discovered the world of baking. But Damien's English was "not good enough" and it became his best excuse for spending most of his nights in the small cellar of my bakery.

We baked sourdough baguettes and levain bread together throughout the nights for some of the finest hotel breakfast buffets in Stockholm. He had, just like me, spent plenty of early mornings with our father and older brother at the bakery and it did not take him long to become one of the team.

Time went by and the small bakery at Stora Essingen grew. Those were wonderful times. But even though we were baking sourdough for the finest establishments in Stockholm, something was still missing in our bakery lives. Petite France was what was missing. I had dreamt for a very long time of a bakery filled with delicious pastries and sourdough that had been leavened for many hours; a café with a warm atmosphere and good food with a line out the door as far as the eyes could see. The dream became reality at John Ericssongatan 6 and it was in big part due to my brother Damien and his amazing macaroons. Without his help, it would never have happened.

What I admire most about Damien is that he has grown within his profession without stealing glances at others for comparison. This has allowed him to create his own individual style. Today, he is one of the best pastry chefs in Sweden. Not because he can make clever sugar sculptures or compose à la carte desserts in fifteen stages, but because he puts his heart and soul into every morsel of whipped cream, egg, and chocolate he touches.

Mom and Dad—you can be proud of the fact that you did end up with an engineer in the family. Damien builds architectural pieces of art every day. He creates bridges between people and uses his powers in the most generous sense there is—to make other people happy. *Merci p'tit frèrot!*

DEATH BY CHOCOLATE

It is not like you'll actually die, but the experience is not far from it. This dessert has the smoothest chocolate cream imaginable and the texture of the chocolate fondant will have you tipping over. Eat it sitting, lying down, or leaning against a wall with a perfectly paired espresso.

12 TARTS

TART CRUST

7 tbsp (3½ oz/100 g) cold butter

1⅔ cups (200 g) wheat flour

3 tbsp (25 g) cocoa powder

½ cup (100 g) sugar

a pinch of fleur de sel (fine sea salt)

1 (1½ oz/40 g) egg

CHOCOLATE FONDANT

⅔ cup (5 oz/150 g) butter

4 oz (120 g) dark chocolate, 70%

5 oz (150 g) milk chocolate

4–5 (3 oz/90 g) egg yolks

½ cup (100 g) sugar

4–5 (4¾ oz/135 g) egg whites

1 batch chocolate ganache (pg. 234)

DAY 1

1. Sift the cold butter between your hands with flour, cocoa, sugar, and salt until you have a grainy consistency. Make sure it does not yet turn into dough.

2. Add the egg and mix until dough is compact. Wrap in plastic and let it rest in the fridge for 12 hours.

DAY 2

1. Preheat the oven to 400°F (200°C).

2. Remove the dough from the fridge and place it on a floured baking table to rest for 15 minutes at room temperature. Thoroughly knead the dough until it has a smooth consistency. Check if it is ready by taking a piece in your hand and pressing your finger into it—if the edges do not crack, it is ready. Wrap the dough in plastic and let it rest in the fridge until it gets cold again.

3. Roll out the dough to just under ⅛ of an inch (2 mm) thick. Cut out small round shapes and place them in the tart molds.

4. Pre bake the tart crusts for 10 minutes. Remove them from the oven and reduce the heat to 285°F (140°C).

5. *Preparing the fondant:* Melt the butter over low heat without letting it boil. Melt the chocolate over a water bath until the chocolate has a temperature of 115–120°F (45–50°C).

6. Whisk the egg yolks and half the sugar in a bowl until the sugar has melted and the mixture is light yellow in color.

7. Add the melted butter into the chocolate. Then, thoroughly stir the egg yolk mixture into the chocolate. Put the mixture aside but make sure it does not cool completely.

8. Whisk the egg whites until it has turned into foam. When the egg whites start to harden, gently add sugar while continuing to whisk. Pour the egg foam into the chocolate mixture and stir until it is elastic and shiny.

9. Fill the tarts halfway with the fondant. Bake for 6–8 minutes in the oven. They're ready if the mixture does not move when you shake the tarts. Remove the tarts from the molds and let them cool completely.

10. Pipe a layer of ganache on top of the tarts.

ÉCLAIR AU CHOCOLAT

A classic that can be made with many different flavors: coffee, pistachio, or plain milk chocolate. Here is a more adult version made with dark chocolate. It's also easy to eat. You barely have to open your mouth.

12 ÉCLAIRS
PATE À CHOUX DOUGH
½ cup (125 g/125 ml) water
½ cup (125 g/125 ml) milk
a pinch of fleur de sel (fine sea salt)
a pinch of sugar
½ cup (4½ oz/25 g) unsalted butter
1¼ cups (150 g) wheat flour
5 (9 oz/250 g) eggs

CHOCOLATE TOPPING
½ cup (100 ml) water
⅔ cup (130 g) sugar
7¾ oz (220 g) coarsely chopped dark
    chocolate, 70%

CRÈME PÂTISSERIE AU CHOCOLAT
1 batch crème pâtisserie up until step 4 (pg. 234)
7¾ oz (220 g) coarsely chopped dark
    chocolate, 70%

1. Preheat the oven to 410°F (210°C).

2. Bring all the ingredients except the flour and eggs for the pâte à choux dough to a boil. Remove the pot from the heat just as it starts to boil.

3. Sift the flour into the mixture and stir forcefully with a wooden spoon. Put the pot back on the burner and continue stirring until the batter is compact and shiny and releases from the edges. Pour the batter into a clean bowl.

4. Mix in the eggs one at a time while stirring forcefully. Each egg should be worked into the batter before adding the next one. When the batter pours from the spoon to create a beak-like shape, it has the right consistency.

5. Sprinkle some flour onto parchment paper. Pour the pâte à choux dough into a pastry bag with a round, smooth pipe, and pipe the dough onto the parchment paper in 5-inch (12 cm) long "sausages." Since they will expand during baking, it is important not to pipe them too close together.

6. Bake the pâte à choux dough for about 30 minutes. Reduce the heat to 400°F (200°C) and open the oven door to let out the steam. Close the door again and bake for another 10 minutes.

7. Boil the water and sugar for the chocolate topping in a pot. Remove it from the burner and let it cool. While it cools, melt the chocolate over a water bath until it reaches 100–120°F (40–50°C).

8. Add the sugar mixture, a little at a time, into the melted chocolate while stirring forcefully with a spatula. Continue until all of the sugar mixture has blended into the chocolate.

9. Prepare crème pâtisserie up until step 4 and add the coarsely chopped chocolate and the butter.

10. *Prepare the éclair:* Create three small holes in the bottom of the pastry with a small pastry bag tip. Turn the tip until you have three clearly defined holes. Pour the chocolate cream into a pastry bag with a small tip and fill the éclair with the chocolate cream.

11. Dip the top of the éclairs in chocolate topping. Let them cool in the fridge for a couple of hours before serving.

LES CRÈMES

Two delightful creams to fill your pastries with. Make them ahead of time and store them in the fridge, tightly sealed in plastic.

CRÈME PÂTISSÈRIE

5 (3½ oz/100 g) egg yolks
2 tbsp (15 g) wheat flour
2 tbsp (15 g) potato flour
1½ tbsp (10 g) corn flour
½ cup (100 g) sugar
1 vanilla bean
2 cups (500 g/500 ml) milk
⅓ cup (2⅔ oz/75 g) unsalted butter at room temperature

1. Whisk the egg yolks with the wheat, potato, and corn flour and half the sugar.
2. Score the vanilla bean lengthwise and scrape out the seeds into a pot along with the bean. Add milk and the rest of the sugar and bring to a boil.
3. Add a small part of the boiling milk into the egg mixture and then pour the rest of the egg mixture into the milk. Bring it to a boil while stirring forcefully.
4. Pour the cream into a bowl. Add the butter and stir with a spatula until the butter has melted.
5. Let the cream cool and then cover with plastic wrap (the plastic should be in direct contact with the cream). Place the bowl in the fridge for a couple hours.

CHOCOLATE GANACHE

4½ oz (130 g) dark chocolate, 70%
4½ oz (130 g) milk chocolate, 40%
1¼ cups (300 g/300 ml) heavy cream
4 tbsp (2 oz/60 g) unsalted butter at room temperature

1. Melt the chocolate over a water bath until it reaches a temperature of 120°F (50°C).
2. Bring the heavy cream to a boil. Pour the hot cream into the chocolate, a little bit at a time (as if you were making mayonnaise), while stirring forcefully with a spatula. Adding small amounts of cream to the chocolate at a time creates a smooth and delicate ganache. *Note:* While you work the cream into the chocolate, the temperature should never reach below 95°F (35°C).
3. Let the ganache cool until it has reached a temperature of 95–100°F (35–40°C). Add the butter and work it into the ganache with a hand mixer. Angle the mixer so that it mixes at the bottom of the bowl; this will prevent any air from entering the ganache.
4. Cover the ganache with plastic wrap (ensuring that the plastic is in direct contact with the cream). Let it rest at room temperature for 2–3 hours until it has solidified. Then place the cream in the fridge.

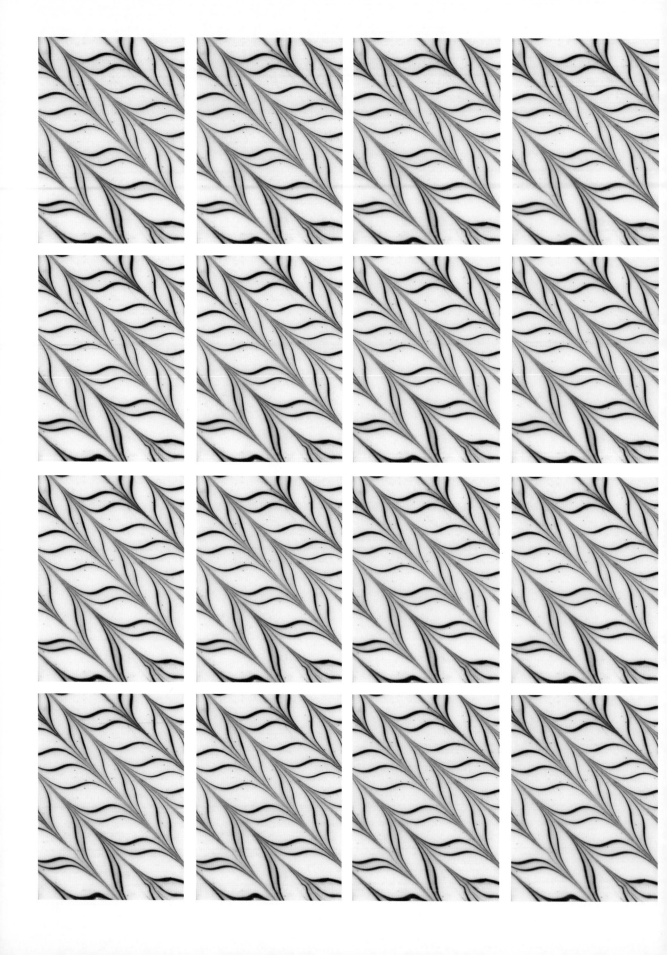

MILLE-FEUILLES

Mille-feuilles means "a thousand leaves." It's a work of art with countless number of layers. It is just as refined as it is simple. Three crisp and flaky layers of melting puff pastry and two layers of smooth and silky crème pâtissière topped off with white icing marbled with Nutella—so simple yet so complicated! If you want to make an easier version, you can omit the marbling and instead sprinkle powdered sugar over your mille-feuilles. Remember to prepare the puff pastry two days ahead of time.

10 PORTIONS
1 batch puff pastry (pg. 194)
1 batch crème pâtissière (pg. 234)
1 tbsp Nutella

ICING
2½ cups (250 g) powdered sugar
3 tbsp (40 g) water
seeds from 1 vanilla bean
a few drops of freshly squeezed lemon juice

1. Preheat the oven to 425°F (220°C).
2. Roll the puff pastry dough onto a floured table until it has become a 12 x 12 inch (30 x 30 cm) square, ⅛ of an inch (2–3 mm) thick.
3. Place the dough on a baking sheet covered with parchment paper and bake in the oven for 25–30 minutes. Press out the air bubbles from the dough while baking by occasionally pressing down on the dough with another baking sheet. Remove the puff pastry from the oven and let it cool.
4. Cut the puff pastry into three even pieces. Spread out half the crème pâtissière over the first puff pastry piece. Place the second piece on top of the first and spread out the remaining cream. Place the third piece on top and press down gently to remove any potential air bubbles.
5. *Prepare the icing:* Heat up the powdered sugar, water, and vanilla seeds in a pot over low heat—the temperature should not exceed 100°F (40°C). Remove the pot from the burner and add the lemon juice.
6. Pour the icing over your mille-feuilles.
7. Create an icing bag from parchment paper by rolling it diagonally, creating a small tip. Fill the bag with Nutella and pipe straight lines diagonally over the icing. Use the back end of a knife to draw diagonal lines in the opposite direction of the Nutella lines at ½-inch (1 cm) widths apart. Next, draw the knife in the opposite direction of the lines to create a beautiful marbled pattern as shown in the picture. It is important to decorate this last step fairly quickly as the icing hardens fast.
8. Let your mille-feuilles rest in the fridge for 2–3 hours before serving.

CRÈME BRÛLÉE

The most recognized French dessert in the world. Not in a new, contemporary way, nor with any weird berries or—even worse—a stem of lemon balm on top. Just a really great recipe for a really great and simple dessert.

6 PORTIONS
2 vanilla beans (preferably from Tahiti)
6 (4¼ oz/120 g) egg yolks
⅔ cups (120 g) sugar
2½ cups (600 g/600 ml) heavy cream, 40%
2–3 lavender flowers
raw sugar for burning

DAY 1

1. Score the vanilla beans lengthwise and scrape out the seeds. Whisk the egg yolks, sugar, and vanilla beans until the sugar has melted. The color should be anything from dark to light yellow and the mixture should be smooth. Add the cream, a little at a time, while you continue whisking.
2. Cover the mixture with plastic wrap and place in the fridge for 12 hours.

DAY 2

1. Preheat the oven to 200°F (100°C).
2. Stir the batter with a spatula to release the vanilla beans from the bottom of the bowl. Divide the mixture into six small baking dishes. Sprinkle 2–3 lavender flowers into each dish. (No more than that, as the flavor is meant to be delicate and gentle. It shouldn't leave a taste of grandma's closet.)
3. Place the dishes on a baking tray with water in it. Bake for about 90 minutes in the middle of the oven (the bigger the baking dish, the longer the baking time). The brûlée is ready when the batter has solidified and is firm when you gently shake the dishes. Remove from the oven and let them cool.
4. Wrap the dishes in plastic and let them rest in the fridge for a few hours.
5. Sprinkle some raw sugar on top of the brûlées and burn the surface with a torch before serving.

"A perfect crème brûlée is smooth and creamy on the inside with the sugar crunchy and golden brown on the outside, leaving your guests silent with delight!"

SUNRISE IN PAU
In the fall of 2011, a group of us working on this book went to Pau in the south of France to take pictures, cook some food, and be inspired to write. Each morning we woke up to this amazing view of the mighty Pyrenees.

INDEX

SUBJECT INDEX

EXTRAS

For a few select recipes within this book, I have made accompanying video clips where I show how to prepare them. To access these clips, visit my blog www.brodpassion.se.

THANK YOU

Lars Fuhre for convincing me to write this book and bringing me to Bonnier Fakta. Thanks to all the readers who follow my blog Brödpassion *and to the whole team at Petite France who helped me realize my dreams. Thank you Jenny Edlund for all your help in France, the vegetable market at Sorunda and all the lovely fruits and veggies, and to everyone at Bageriprodukter. Thanks to Eva Bratell and Mats Carlsson for lending us the house at Solsidan, Andrea, and Johan Wallenburg for Yellow House in Jurançon, Jacky Otto-Bruc for lending us the bakery in Blois, Niklas, and Joakim Blomqvist from Mariannes Fish, Leif and Lennart Nyman at Orga Mill, La Ferme Landaise, Caroline Düringer and Caroline at Choklade Compagniet. Thank you to Evelina Kleiner, Modesto Saraguro "le chef," DN På Stan for all the awards, Hanna Wik, lovely Zoë Lagache for the pain au chocolat picture, Mats Larsson for the cheeses and even more than that. Thanks Peter Hartai for adopting my child Petite France, Xavier Dubost and Eva Tiselius for all your help. Per Wivall for managing this project so well. Olaf Hajek for your fantasy and talent, Julia Hallengren for treating our photography with love. Last but not least, a big thank you to Justine, Hanna, and Calle. Mes trois mousequetaires! Great wheat, great baker, great bread, the best of friends, with all my love—this book.*

Skyhorse Publishing books may be purchased in bulk at special discounts for sales promotion, corporate gifts, fund-raising, or educational purposes. Special editions can also be created to specifications. For details, contact the Special Sales Department, Skyhorse Publishing, 307 West 36th Street, 11th Floor, New York, NY 10018 or info@skyhorsepublishing.com.

Skyhorse® and Skyhorse Publishing® are registered trademarks of Skyhorse Publishing, Inc.®, a Delaware corporation.

www.skyhorsepublishing.com

10 9 8 7 6 5 4 3 2 1

Library of Congress Cataloging-in-Publication Data is available on file.

ISBN: 978-1-62087-999-3

Printed in China

CONVERSION TABLE

INGREDIENT	<⅓ CUP	1 TBSP	1 TSP
Water	100 g	15 g	5 g
Heavy cream	100 g	15 g	5 g
Wheat flour	60 g	9 g	3 g
Almond flour	60 g	9 g	
Potato flour	80 g	12 g	4 g
Stone-ground rye flour	60 g	10 g	
Corn flour	55 g	8 g	3 g
Organic oats	45 g	4–5 g	
Rye grains	45 g	4–5 g	
Flax seeds	65 g	10 g	
Pistachio nuts	65 g	10 g	
Pumkin seeds	65 g	10 g	
Sesame seeds	70 g	12 g	
Sunflower seeds	75 g	13 g	
Raw sugar	90 g	12 g	
Conventional sugar	85 g	12 g	
Fleur de sel (fine sea salt)		12 g	4 g
Coarse sea salt	120 g	18 g	6 g
1 organic egg	50 g		
1 organic egg yolk	20 g		
1 organic egg white	30 g		